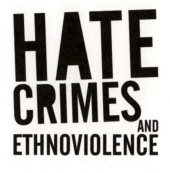

HATE CRIMES AND ETHNOVIOLENCE

HATE CRIMES
AND
ETHNOVIOLENCE

The History, Current Affairs, and
Future of Discrimination in America

ESSAYS BY

HOWARD J. EHRLICH

The Prejudice Institute

Westview
PRESS

A Member of the Perseus Books Group

Designed by Trish Wilkinson
Set in 11-point Minion

A CIP catalog record for this book is available from the Library of Congress
ISBN-13: 978-08133-4445-4

10 9 8 7 6 5 4 3 2 1

To Pat,
who enriched my life and made this all possible

CONTENTS

PART IV
THE STRUGGLE CONTINUES

PREFACE
The Ethnoviolence Project

It began in 1985 with two signal events: a massive desecration of a synagogue in Silver Spring, Maryland, and a substantial rally and march by the Ku Klux Klan in southern Maryland. The then governor, Harry Hughes, shocked by these episodes, ordered the formation of a commission to propose a course of action. The commission made two recommendations. One was the chartering of a statewide survey to assess public attitudes. The survey was conducted and concluded that teenagers were the major, and growing, source of prejudice in the state. The findings were specious, but they scared the hell out of policymakers and the commission. The commission's second, more notable action was to recommend that the governor form a nonprofit institute and provide seed money for three years to address the issues of prejudice and violence. After three years, the institute was to become self-supporting. The newly formed board of directors fantasized that state governors around the country would recognize the need for such an organization and provide financial support, while the executive director's fantasy was that large business corporations would also provide financial support. Of course neither the states nor big business had any real commitment to the project.

The following year I joined the Prejudice Institute as its research director. One of my first tasks was to generate a research agenda. Given our small size (nine people at our peak) and mainly soft-money budget, it was my belief that our major contribution would come by designing small studies and concept papers at the cutting edge of research. I coined the term *ethnoviolence* to demarcate our mission—the study of violence motivated by prejudice. It wasn't until four years later that the term *hate crimes* became part of the lexicon of prejudice. As you shall see in succeeding chapters, the differences between ethnoviolence and hate crimes have had exceptional implications for research and social policy. These differences are highlighted by the conflicts between a sociological paradigm and a set of legal statutes.

This book is a collection of the studies and papers I wrote during my tenure with the Prejudice Institute. They are held together by an underlying, complex theme: the manifestations of prejudice, that is, negative attitudes towards a group (or a person) because of their group membership. I believe that prejudice is almost always a necessary condition of ethnoviolence, although the link between the two is not always obvious.

To understand prejudice and ethnoviolence fully, you need to place them in their sociohistorical context. As I say in the opening chapter, no one can grow up in this society without learning the dominant group stereotypes and the norms of social discrimination. This is a part of our social heritage, and in Chapter 1 I look at the dimensions of this heritage as they have changed from the1950s through the beginning of the twenty-first century. The ten dimensions I introduce, taken together, form a unique context in which to study ethnoviolence.

In Chapters 2 and 3, I focus on explaining the difference between ethnoviolence and hate crimes and present an overview of research findings in this area, with special emphasis on the forms and prevalence of ethnoviolence, its perpetrators, and the traumatic effects of victimization. Chapter 3 is premised on the belief that ethnoviolence and hate crimes are about issues of power—the ability of a dominant group to maintain its authority through physical and psychological modes of oppression.

In Part II, I shift to an examination of the news media and expose how they are a primary source for teaching and maintaining racial and ethnic attitudes and justifying many forms of discrimination. I present the basic features of a media environment model by which we can better comprehend the centrality of the news media in maintaining intergroup relations.

Chapter 5 concentrates on the gatekeepers of newspaper reports of race and ethnic relations. I look at how the editor as an institutional representative chooses reporters assigned to cover stories of race and ethnicity, and how editors view beat reporting in this arena and view group relations in the community. This is based on my interviews with editors of the forty-eight leading circulating newspapers in the country.

The editors' study is followed by interviews with two samples of reporters. I spoke with experienced general-assignment reporters and equally experienced reporters assigned to what was essentially a race and ethnic beat. (Newspapers have different names for the beat but they were basically a race beat.) I looked at who these two groups of reporters are, their training, how they view the problems of civil rights and ethnoviolence, their conflicts with editors, and the effects all this has on them personally. As you will see, the differences between the two groups of reporters, aside from the fact that the beat reporters were more likely to be black women, was their level of conflict. As one beat reporter said of her editor, "He wants me to write white."

In Chapters 6 and 7, I switch to an examination of television news and present the findings of our unique study of thirteen late-evening local newscasts in twelve cities around the country. I look at the structure and content of the news stories and how that intersects with race, ethnicity, and gender. In doing so, I focus on the portrayal of major characters and authority figures in the stories. I conclude by placing the data in the context of social capital—that is, the contribution of the newscast to the well-being of the community.

Four spectacular events became part of American popular culture in the past two decades: the bombing of a federal building in Oklahoma City, the civic disorders in Los Angeles in 1992, the Columbine High School shootings, and the events surrounding Hurricane Katrina. Each event had different but deep-reaching effects on intergroup relations. In Part III, Chapter 8, I look at the role of the political elites and the way the news media transformed these events into something beyond themselves. For each event, I identify its teachable moments and the lessons we should have learned. In the following chapter, I focus on the college campus as the site of a culture of prejudice and ethnoviolence. The materials presented here are based on five national surveys and approximately forty campus case studies.

In the final part of the book, Chapter 10 presents a checklist for identifying right-wing influences on discrimination and ethnoviolence. I use a checklist form to emphasize that right and left are not the poles of a single continuum. Recognizing the multidimensional character of the right helps us better comprehend the underlying structure of their ideologies.

As an educator and activist, I have become increasingly concerned with political ignorance as a tool of oppression. I emphasize in Chapter 11 the attributes of political ignorance: it is shared (that is, many people hold the information in common and share it with others); the shared information is false or misleading; and the information distracts people from autonomous and democratic behavior. In the final chapter of the book, I address what we need to do to develop an egalitarian society.

I end with a personal and political look at the concentration of power and the recognition that no resolve exists among the political, business, educational, or religious elites regarding principles of social justice or an equitable economy. I argue that to achieve social justice, we need institutions that meld a participatory democracy with a participatory economy, minimizing power differentials and optimizing self-management.

ACKNOWLEDGMENTS

These materials, the ideas and the research, were facilitated over the years by interns, volunteers, secretaries, and my colleagues at the original National Institute Against Prejudice & Violence and its successor, the Prejudice Institute.

Chapters 5, 6, and 7 were completed with the financial support of the Annie E. Casey Foundation and by the SAGES award from the Society for the Psychological Study of Social Issues (SPSSI).

In particular I want to thank the following people:

Adam Bookman, Stacey Bouchet, Charles Brown, Andrew Burkhardt, Laura Carlson, Melissa Childs, Mary DeFreest, Allison Doherty, Allison Eden, Ari Fogelman, Rachel Forbes, Caroline Hailey, Brian Hammock, Stephanie Heard, Naoko Kawamura, Juliana P. W. Kerrest, Julia Kim, Megan Kreider, Debbie Lacy, Barbara E. K. Larcom, Kathryn Lynch, Carolina Martin, Robert Purvis, Raquel J. Saavedra, Ericka Schmeckpecker, Jolanta Smolen, Karen Taylor, Frank Tisano, Andrea Torres, Laura Turner, Jason Weller, Valene Whittaker, Liz Wiemers, Summer Woo.

PART I

ETHNOVIOLENCE

1

THE SOCIAL CONDITIONS
OF ETHNOVIOLENCE

"If you continue along this path," a Cherokee maxim cautions, "you will get where you are going." The path we are on has neither been anticipated nor appraised with any exactitude. There are two solid reasons for this: social amnesia and denial. Americans seem not to remember their history very well, and they deny those parts of history that do not fit the prevailing ideology.

The denial and amnesia of American intergroup relations tends to be psychological. We look at the perpetrator of an ethnoviolent act and say, for example, that he acted out of anger and simply has an antisocial personality. We could have said that the perpetrator acted in the context of a major and rapid influx of a culturally different minority due to the potential loss of his own status. The two explanations are complementary, but they lead the policymaker in different directions. The former focuses on the personality of the perpetrator. The latter focuses on the social conditions that lead to the prejudice-motivated behavior of the perpetrator. In this chapter we focus on the major social conditions that lead to prejudice, discrimination, and ethnoviolence.

There are ten pathways that brought us to where we are. We begin at the beginning:

- The social heritage of prejudice and discrimination
- The incorporation of violence into everyday behavior
- Rapid social and economic change
- Economic restructuring of the 1980s and 1990s

- Globalization
- The culture of denial
- Power and social class
- The growth of corporate power
- Bureaucracy
- The selling of self-worthlessness

THE SOCIAL HERITAGE OF PREJUDICE AND DISCRIMINATION

The first pathway is the *heritage of prejudice and discrimination in society.* We need to make this observation explicit: Every child comes to learn the traditions and norms of the society he or she is born into. Prejudice and discrimination are part of those traditions and norms. They are part of our cultural heritage. Not everyone accepts this part of the cultural heritage, but no one can escape dealing with it. Social psychologists have documented that children begin to learn group prejudices by the ages of three and four—before they even have the capacity to distinguish between groups. Because virtually all children learn these prevailing attitudes and norms, they have to unlearn them to progress. Even so, these attitudes are part of the culture and in that regard are constantly primed and to some degree retained as filters through which we still occasionally observe and classify people and groups.

THE INCORPORATION OF VIOLENCE INTO EVERYDAY BEHAVIOR

The second pathway defines violence as commonplace. Violence is inescapable even within the family. Family violence is the leading cause of injury to women, and the physical punishment of children is common and for some young people does not end until they leave home.

In the past twenty years we have seen the growth of random mass shootings, not to ignore terrorist violence. Even more bizarre are incidents where perpetrator and victim have nothing in common.

In the home, television multiplies the models of violence that people, and especially children, are exposed to. According to an American Psychological Association report, the average child will see eight thousand murders on television before finishing elementary school. And this does not account for all the other forms of physical and psychological violence that are routinely depicted.

As violence is increasingly modeled in all dimensions of life, people have come to include a violent response as a behavioral option. With violence incorporated into one's personal repertoire, the likelihood of a violent act increases.

RAPID SOCIAL AND ECONOMIC CHANGE

The third of these conditions is *rapid social and economic change*. The 1950s are an appropriate starting point for assessing changes in intergroup relations. This decade marked the start of desegregation in schools and public accommodations as well as the growth of the civil rights movement. It marked also the start of the cold war and the beginning of the national security state as well as forty years of hot wars.

Compared to the turn of the twentieth century, the United States in 1950 was a more decentralized manufacturing society, highly individualistic, and believed strongly in small business free enterprise. The central city was the focus of residence and business. The cold war of the 1950s muffled dissent, driving communists and political deviants into the closet and creating a new pattern of growth for the political right wing.

Today the country is a bureaucratized agglomeration of centralized business centered on information processing and the provision of services. The population has shifted to the suburbs and many older cities are in a state of decline. In 1960, for example, the population was equally divided between cities, suburbs, and rural areas. By 1990, suburbs accounted for half the population. As cities lost population they became economically poorer and more minority in composition. As the population shifted, so did the federal government's contribution to cities.

The rapid growth in suburbs continues. The shift to suburbanization accompanied a greater privatization of the family and residence. New technologies such as the video recorder, cable and satellite television, and more recently the Internet and other online services have added to that isolation. In the 1950s, visiting families and friends was the major leisure time activity of Americans. Today, it is watching television and other home-based activities. This withdrawal is manifest also in the growth of gated communities, which by some estimates have over four million residents, and the growth of private community associations, which contain close to fifty million people (Community Association Institute, 2006). Guarding these homes and workplaces is an army of private police that already outnumbers public police agencies. These developments have obvious strong implications for intergroup contacts and relationships.

By the 1950s, it became apparent that the women who had left home to work in the defense industries of the war would not return. Patriarchy was challenged. African Americans moved from the rural south, where they had been resettled as slaves, to the urban centers of the north and west, and then demanded equal rights under the law. White supremacy was challenged. More recently, gays and lesbians came out of the closet, and heterosexuality was challenged.

By the 1960s, television had brought the world to American homes. The sixties saw the first televised war (the American war in Indochina) and the modeling of violence on prime-time television. The movements for social change that flourished in the late sixties had lasting consequences: the development of a new political consciousness with a strong commitment to egalitarianism and democratic activism. However, the strong radical and countercultural trends of the new left of that period, which extended through the early 1970s, so threatened traditional values and existing power arrangements that a serious opposition developed. The new left created the new right; and the rest of this decade, extending through the presidential administrations of Reagan, Bush, and Clinton, saw the rise of a powerful conservative movement and a new era of rightist, white supremacist organizations. By the end of the 1980s, America had become politically polarized, and that polarization continues today.

With the end of the war in Indochina in the early 1970s and steady growth in inflation and unemployment, the affluence, optimism, and activism of the previous decade dissipated. The 1970s witnessed what some observers termed a mean-spirited reaction to the liberal reformist programs of the 1960s (civil rights acts, Medicare, and massive programs of educational assistance). The altruism of that decade was replaced by a "me-first" orientation that carried with it a rejection of programs designed to help African Americans and the poor.

The pace of social changes increased in the 1980s. Particularly important to an understanding of intergroup relations was the rapid immigration of people from non-English-speaking cultures. These newcomers were, in order of population size, Mexicans, Filipinos, South Koreans, Vietnamese, Indians, and Chinese. Monoculturalism and the metaphor of the melting pot had been challenged. Islam became the fastest growing religion in the United States, and conservatives and the right-wing white supremacist movement began to redefine Christianity. As part of that redefinition, the new Christian right began to organize, overtly and covertly, in the political arena. This added to the polarization of society.

ECONOMIC RESTRUCTURING OF THE 1980S AND 1990S

The fourth pathway is *the economic restructuring of the 1980s and 1990s.* By the 1980s, America's occupational and income structure began to change. The major areas of growth in new jobs were in lower-paying industries, while substantial numbers of higher-paying jobs were made obsolete or exported. As the composition of the workforce shifted, blue-collar factory, transportation, and construction jobs declined drastically, perhaps as much as 70 percent, in the 1970s and 1980s. The effect was greatest among the working-age male black population and was, perhaps, one of the two most important factors in the ghettoization and pauperization of the central city black population.[1] Homelessness and poverty became endemic, and by the late 1990s some social scientists estimated that while the official poverty rate was 16 percent, poverty really affected one in four Americans. The official rates were double for blacks and Hispanics. Approximately 26 million Americans relied on food pantries, soup kitchens, and emergency feeding programs during 1993.[2]

Perhaps for the first time in American history, the size of the middle class began to shrink, threatening the dreams and myths of social mobility of earlier generations. In fact, the U.S. Department of Labor projects that through the first decade of the twenty-first century, 30 percent of each college graduating class will march up the aisle straight to unemployment.

In the opening years of the 1990s, the United States lost an average of one million jobs a year. Part-time and temporary workers reached a new high, amounting to one out of every four workers in 1993. Unemployment among white-collar workers doubled between the early eighties and the early nineties. The American blue-collar worker had already been rendered obsolescent.

The workforce and the character of work changed. The term *downsizing* entered our vocabulary. The Department of Labor estimates that nearly half of American businesses reduced their workforce in the 1990s. Overtime increased (by 4.7 days) and paid vacations decreased (by 3.5 days). The average worker today is doing the work of 1.3 people.[3]

Americans in 2005 were spending more but getting less for their dollar, saving less, and increasing their debt. More and more people slipped into bankruptcy. According to the United Food and Commercial Workers Union, one quarter of all full-time workers earned $8.70 an hour. This is $18,100 annually, approximately the poverty level for a family of four in the United States. Whereas the Commerce Department estimated a poverty rate in the United States of 13 percent, a United Nations survey estimated a true rate close to 50 percent. Poverty increased every year of this new century, with Latinos moving into poverty at a faster rate than blacks or whites.

While the rate of inflation slowed down by the turn of the century, the inflation-adjusted income of workers today is almost one-fifth of what it was twenty years before. The average chief executive officer was paid $11.8 million a year in 2004, according to the Institute for Policy Studies. In stark contrast, the average worker (at $27,460 a year) earns $1 for every $431 paid to the CEO.

GLOBALIZATION

The dominant trend of this economic restructuring has been *globalization,* the fifth pathway. The political geographer David Harvey defines the underlying ideology of globalization as follows:

> Neoliberalism is in the first instance a theory of political economic practices that proposes that human well-being can best be advanced by liberating individual entrepreneurial freedoms and skills within an institutional framework characterized by strong private property rights, free markets, and free trade. The role of the state is to create and preserve an institutional framework appropriate to such practices.[4]

The global economy means that goods and even services can be produced anywhere and sold anywhere. It means that American corporations are shifting their production overseas to places with cheaper labor. Globalization is characterized by a devaluation of the regulatory capability of the state and an increase in the power of the corporate sector. It involves the privatization of public services and the decrease of democratic processes.

Globalization robs society of its social capital. It increases hierarchy, concentrates power, and promotes individualism. The consequences are the disenfranchisement and unemployment of the working and lower-middle class, especially black and brown workers.

THE CULTURE OF DENIAL

There is a pervasive hostility to the often inadequate attempts of government to deal with continuing discrimination and the new wave of ethnoviolence. Noticeably lacking is any national resolve among religious leaders or business or political elites to deal with the difficulties besetting intergroup relations. Many Americans do not believe that antiminority discrimination is even a major problem. This *culture of denial,* our sixth pathway, is the social condition contributing to the persistence of prejudice, discrimination, and conflict. Like all cultural patterns, these are transmitted across families, friends, and teachers, and authorized and maintained by authorities in the government, the church, and the mass media. Evidence can be seen in such occasions as President Ronald Reagan's assertion that civil rights leaders exaggerate racial problems to keep their organizations alive.[5] The purpose of this presidential pronouncement was to tell the country that there were no racial problems of serious concern. In other cases, the issue goes unmentioned and thus does not become part of the public agenda. For example, despite four days of intergroup violence in Los Angeles (29 April through 2 May 1992), race and ethnic-group relations were not on the agenda of the major philanthropic foundations in the country; indeed, one would be hard-pressed to create a substantial list of business, political, or religious elites who have been outspoken in their support of such programs.

One factor underlying this "official" denial has been the response of the American public. National polls reveal that nearly one out of every two white Americans believes that blacks are as well off as whites or have the same opportunities in life. (Less than one out of five blacks holds the same belief.) In fact, the relative disadvantage of blacks has held stable throughout history and in many cases can still be described as extreme—in health, housing, income, and justice, among other comparisons.

The culture of denial has so permeated American society that it has deeply influenced the way many whites think about prejudice. Many white people deny that discrimination against minorities persists and thus conclude that any interventions designed to equalize opportunities are uncalled for. In some cases, such interventions (for example, affirmative action and relaxed immigration) are viewed as disadvantaging whites. This line of thought has resulted in an increased polarization of blacks, browns, and whites in a growing white opposition to programs of social action. It has also become central to the appeals of the right-wing white supremacist movement, which defines the differences that do exist as cultural and calls for the preservation of a white-only society and a halt to immigration to maintain a "true Christian American" culture.

POWER AND SOCIAL CLASS

The seventh social condition contributing to the development of prejudice and its manifestation as discrimination, conflict, and ethnoviolence concerns *social class and power in society*. Americans vary widely in terms of their life chances, which in turn are determined by the resources of power that people have at their disposal as individuals or as members of a group. It is our premise that the greater the differences of power in a society, the greater the discrimination against minorities. Such power differentials are maintained through social class membership and bureaucratic organization.

The social class system is built on differences in wealth and power and the lifestyles that accompany those differences. The question of how social classes persist is a central problem of sociology and, indeed, one of the reasons for its persistence is relevant here. People are socialized to accept the basic structures and norms of their society. And most Americans believe that our class system is basically fair—that the differences in wealth and power among people have been justly brought about and that it is appropriate for families to pass along their privileges to their children.

However, although most people appear to accept the class system, the *extent* to which inequalities characterize the social classes is generally regarded as unfair. For example, many people would describe as unfair the fact that in 1991 the average chief executive officer of a large corporation earned as much as 104 factory workers, and that in 1992 more than twice as many black infants as white infants died before they were one year old. There is an underlying tension about the American class system, but this tension is mediated by the belief—some would say mythological belief—that anyone can achieve wealth and power through individual efforts. It is mediated as well by a deeply rooted fear of alternatives to the political and economic design of American society, a fear fostered by those who most benefit from its present structure.

The inequalities among social classes are closely connected to those among ethnic groups. The parallels are twofold. First, minority Americans occupy a disproportionate number of lower-middle, working-class, and lower-class positions. Because of the considerable overlap between class and color and other ethnic identifications, accepting the class system as legitimate and fair is equivalent to accepting the system of minority stratification as legitimate and fair.

Second, the class system fosters the development of prejudice, discrimination, and conflict because it is a system of inequality. From a social-psychological perspective, treating people differently because of ethnicity or class has the same underlying dynamic. A fundamental contradiction exists between economic inequality and the acceptance of racial and ethnic equality. This is the built-in paradox of modern society.

THE GROWTH OF CORPORATE POWER

Our next pathway is the *growth of corporate power.* Corporate welfare is greater than poverty welfare.[6] The Center for the Study of Responsive Law estimates that the federal government provides tax breaks and subsidies—that is, corporate welfare—in the amount of $167 billion annually. The comparable figure for public welfare programs such as food stamps, aid to families with dependent children, housing subsidies, and the like does not exceed $50 billion. Crime in the suites exceeds crime in the streets. For example, Americans will be paying off the savings and loan failure of the late 1980s and early 1990s until the year 2020.

Corporate welfare began in the late 1800s when the U.S. Supreme Court effectively ruled that under the Fourteenth amendment corporations had "personhood." This definition, which gave citizenship to persons born or naturalized in the United States, ironically transmogrified this strange, amoral paper organizational form into a person. As "persons," corporations became invested with virtually all the legal rights of real people, including the right to equal protection and free speech. Corporations became relatively immune to the consequences of their crimes, wreaking violence against people in all institutional areas from medicine and the environment to the mass production of cars and the mass agglomeration of telemarketers. The National Lawyers Guild in a brief against Nike cited Marjorie Kelly's book *The Divine Right of Capital*: "Why have the rich gotten richer while employee income has stagnated? Because that's the way the corporation is designed."

Aren't there socially responsible companies? The best estimate is that they amount to one-hundredth of 1 percent of the sales of all enterprises worldwide.[7]

Corporatization has become especially important in the new century for at least three solid reasons. First, it subverts democracy through its concentrated wealth and ability to "buy" legislation and elections. Second, it is central to the prevailing neoliberal economics being played out in globalization. Third, corporatization requires a bureaucratic organizational form (more about this in the next section).

More recently, corporate capitalism has expanded to encompass education. The charter school movement has become a new base for investment. This was supplemented in the year 2000 by the "No Child Left Behind" legislation. While benign in appearance—after all, who could oppose tutoring poor students in reading and math—the legislation will lead to more charter and other private schools. Furthermore, as major corporations come to control schools, they will also come to control curricula and social attitudes. Granting personhood to corporations is ultimately subversive of democracy.

BUREAUCRACY

Bureaucracy, our ninth pathway, requires that participants accept two basic principles of organization. One is the necessity for some people to have power and authority over others. The other is the requirement that participants accept an impersonal orientation; that is, people can be treated as objects. Those in authority in a bureaucratic organization therefore have a license to manipulate the behavior and lives of others without regard to their identity as individuals.[8] Such depersonalization is a necessary condition of discrimination and ethnoviolence.

There is a double irony to the development of the organizational form. Originally, bureaucracy was heralded as a rational succession to other forms of authority—to theocracies, monarchies, rule by charismatic leaders, and nepotism. It was seen as a way of rationalizing social control. However, it has evolved as a major means of social control that in its own way is more violent than the organizational forms it replaced.

Participation in a bureaucratic organization has the effect of validating inequality and authorizing depersonalization as an acceptable mode of behavior and of subjecting people to the repeated experience of treating others in this manner.

Characteristic of bureaucratic functioning is the absence of personal responsibility. The role of the bureaucrat requires that people be treated uniformly and in an effectively neutral manner. As long as the functionaries remain within the rules and regulations of the organization, they are not personally accountable for the consequences of their bureaucratic acts. This bureaucratic organization socializes all of us into a form of interpersonal violence that reinforces prejudice and is easily adaptable to situations of ethnoviolence.

THE SELLING OF SELF-WORTHLESSNESS

These pathways have a deep, defining influence on what may be called—to use an older term—American national character. As individuals, Americans don't like themselves. I encountered one of the first signs of this some thirty years ago while interviewing a seventeen-year-old Cherokee woman. She had just left the reservation and was enrolled in a Baltimore high school. I was looking for elements of culture shock in her experience, and I asked her what were the most surprising things she had encountered in school. Without hesitation she expressed her bewilderment at her schoolmates: "They don't know who they are. They just don't like themselves." She went on to tell me how comfortable the traditional society she had come from was. Everyone had a place, and they knew their place.

Her comments left an indelible impression on me because of a startling coincidence. I had been writing a book on the social psychology of prejudice and had just completed a section on self attitudes, and here was someone anticipating what I introduce as the tenth and final pathway on our journey: *the selling of self-worthlessness.*

Two basic principles of prejudice are that people who have negative attitudes toward themselves tend to have negative attitudes toward others, and that negative attitudes are generalized, that is, people who are prejudiced toward one group tend to be prejudiced toward many groups. Thus, one way to work at reducing prejudice is to work at increasing self-acceptance. The converse is also the case. If you increase the level of self-rejection, you increase the individual's level of prejudice.

Advertising, one of the largest industries in the United States, with an annual gross approaching $3 billion, maintains an underlying theme of self-worthlessness. Central to their persuasive message is a subtle appeal. You (the reader or viewer) are seriously inadequate. You drive the wrong car, use the wrong deodorant, wear the wrong clothes, drink the wrong beer, and on and on. You are bordering on worthless (although this can be cured by buying the right product). The constant exposure to such appeals is manifestly effective.

Another component of self-rejection is personal isolation. These two are likely reciprocally related. As isolation increases, self-rejection increases; as self-rejection increases, isolation increases. McPherson, Smith-Lovin, and Brashears examined the social networks of Americans in 1985 and 2004, asking, among other questions, "Who are the people with whom you discuss matters important to you?"[9] What they found was that in 1985 the modal number of confidants was three. In 2004, the modal respondent reported having no confidants. This isolation in combination with self-rejection is toxic. It increases people's susceptibility to authoritarian appeals and disengages them from a democratic practice.

SUMMARY

American society has clearly changed rapidly and dramatically since the civil rights movement of the 1950s. For many, this has resulted in a sense of alienation: They feel confused about the new norms of behavior and powerless in such a changing world. Many others have responded by reaffirming their value orientations, which range from one end of the political spectrum to the other. In this social context, Americans are confused by the issues of ethnic-group relations and ethnoviolence has become an acceptable behavioral option.

In this opening survey I have tried to depict the path that guides this country's direction. It should be apparent that if we remain on this path we will not arrive at the democratic, socially just society we thought we were heading towards. We can forge new pathways only by blazing a new trail.

NOTES

1. William Julius Wilson, *When Work Disappears: The World of the New Urban Poor* (Chicago: University of Chicago Press, 1996).

2. *Associated Press,* 9 March 1994.

3. *Newsweek,* 6 March 1995, 60.

4. David Harvey, *A Brief History of Neoliberalism* (Oxford, UK: Oxford University Press, 2005), 2.

5. CBS News, *60 Minutes,* 15 January 1989.

6. Marjorie Kelly, *The Divine Right of Capital: Dethroning the Corporate Aristocracy* (San Francisco: Berrett-Koehler, 2001); Sam Pizzagati, *The Maximum Wage* (New York: Apex Press, 1992); Mark Zepezauer, *Take the Rich Off Welfare* (Cambridge, MA: Sound End Press, 2004).

7. Paul Hawken, *Utne Reader,* September–October, 1993, 54.

8. Harold Pepinsky, *Geometry of Violence and Democracy* (Bloomington: Indiana University Press,1991).

9. Miller McPherson, Lynn Smith-Lovin, and Matthew Brashears, "Social Isolation in America: Changes in Core Discussion Networks Over Two Decades," *American Sociological Review* 71 (June 2006), 353–375.

2

ETHNOVIOLENCE AND HATE CRIMES

WHAT IS ETHNOVIOLENCE?

Ethnoviolence is an act or attempted act motivated by group prejudice with the intention to cause physical or psychological injury. These violent acts include intimidation, harassment, group insults, property defacement or destruction, and physical attacks. The targets of these acts are persons identified because of their race or skin color, gender, nationality or national origin, religion, sexual orientation, or other physical or social characteristic of groups defined to be socially significant.

Ethnoviolence Versus Hate Crimes

The term *hate crime* was developed for legislative and political reasons. It refers to statutorily delimited acts that are conventionally recognized as serious crimes, such as murder, manslaughter, rape, assault, robbery, burglary, arson, some forms of property damage, and some acts of intimidation.

Hate crimes became part of the public and sociological lexicon with the agitation for the passage of a federal hate crimes statute. As the lobbying began in 1985 and 1986, the national media database, Nexis, recorded only eleven and fourteen mentions, respectively. By 1990, with the passage of the Hate Crimes Statistics Act, over five hundred citations were indexed. By the end of the decade, there may have been close to fourteen thousand mentions.[1] Clearly the term had arrived, achieving acceptance by the media and, regrettably, by many social scientists who should have known better. The

17

term *ethnoviolence* had its origin in a small report I wrote for the National Institute Against Prejudice and Violence in 1986.

It is important to look at the differences between the two concepts. This is not an academic exercise in post-modernist analysis. These terms make different claims about the nature of group conflict and about social policy. "Constructing a successful social problem," Donileen Loseke tells us in her textbook on constructionist perspectives, "requires that audiences be convinced that a condition exists, that this condition is troublesome and widespread, that it can be changed, and that it should be changed."[2]

For the criminological claimants, the issues are crime and law and social control. For the "race and ethnic relations" (R&E) claimants, the issues are prejudice and discrimination and the reduction of group tensions. Given the control function of the mass media, through which such claims are legitimated, and the more conservative orientation of criminology, the R&E claimants lost the popular but not the professional contestation. The first round of books published following the popularization of hate crimes were Milton Kleg's *Hate Prejudice and Racism* (Albany: State University of New York Press, 1993) and Jack Levin and Jack McDevitt's *Hate Crimes—The Rising Tide of Bigotry and Bloodshed* (NY: Plenum Press, 1993). Kleg's work is focused on prejudice and discrimination as well as a detailed examination of "hate groups" and two chapters on the role of education in changing attitudes and behavior. In Levin and McDevitt, you will not find any index entries or formal concern with prejudice and discrimination, but there are chapters on the law and the police. Neither book deals with the process and trauma of victimization, which has been a characteristic of the field. Kleg analyzes the sociocultural context and the education of the dominant society, while McDevitt and Levin hone in on the characteristics of perpetrators and how the law enforcement system deals with them.

What's Hate Got to Do with It?

One of the standard phrases of today's white supremacists is that they are not motivated by hate for others but rather by their "love" for their own race (or sometimes put, "their own kind"). We should not dismiss that protest out of hand. The calculated act of intimidation designed to achieve the specific ends of a perpetrator may well reflect psychopathology but not necessarily hate. The implication that all crimes motivated by prejudice involve hate is an empirical matter, not a definitional one. In fact, hate as a strong, intense, negative emotional response is not necessarily involved in so-called hate crimes. Many ethnoviolent incidents are committed impulsively or as acts of peer group conformity.

Among other critics, Andrew Sullivan, the *New York Times Magazine* writer, uses the mislabeling of prejudice-motivated incidents as hate crimes as premise for discounting the entire field. Despite his misconstruction of intergroup relations, his comments on hate are cogent.

The truth is, the distinction between a crime filled with personal hate and a crime filled with group hate is an essentially arbitrary one. It tells us nothing interesting about the psychological contours of the specific actor or his specific victim. It is a function primarily of politics, of special interest groups carving out special protections for themselves, rather than a serious response to a serious criminal concern. In such an endeavor, advocates of hate-crime law cram an entire world of human motivations into an immutable, tiny box called hate and hope they have solved a problem. But nothing has been solved; and some harm may even have been done.

NEUTRALIZING HATE

Stung by the critics, hate crime advocates have begun to shift to the term *bias crime.* Clearly an improvement, the term nevertheless still leaves people mired in the verbal confines of *crime.* That, in turn, has led to the conceptualization of *bias incidents,* which now brings us close to the concept of ethnoviolence. Distinguishing bias crimes and bias incidents may be important for some purposes, but it leaves me unsatisfied on two counts. First, I want analysts to know that we are talking about a matter of intergroup relations and not merely about illegal or illicit behavior. Second, I reject the antiseptic character of this pair of terms. I chose *ethnoviolence* because I wanted to emphasize that we are looking at violent acts, acts that are committed to inflict psychological or physical harm to another person and to do so because of prejudice.

RECOGNIZING ETHNOVIOLENCE

Counting ethnoviolent acts is not as difficult as you might expect. To begin with, perpetrators usually announce their motives verbally or by the use of easily recognized symbols of group prejudice. Here is a short list of identifying marks:

- The use of recognized symbols, slogans or words of group insult
- Posting or circulating leaflets, including the literature of right-wing extremist groups, containing insulting and intimidating statements
- Defacing or destroying property that is publicly associated with a particular group
- Acts that occur on or follow holidays or special events associated with a particular group
- Acts that fit a pattern of past attacks on the target group
- The general consensus of the community that this was an act motivated by prejudice

I have omitted one category of identification: the victim's definition of the situation that the act was motivated by prejudice. From the standpoint of the sincere beliefs of and genuine trauma inflicted on the victim, violence has been done. Further, we need to take that perception and let it guide us to investigate further. It is the tragedy of minority group membership that too many times one never really knows whether the cause of an insult or injury was personal or political.

Another apparent problem is that of hoaxes, that is, acts that appear to be motivated by prejudice but use the symbols of bigotry as a means to a different end. My own guess, after having monitored ethnoviolent incidents for twenty years, is that—at the most—fewer than 2 percent are hoaxes. Sadly, many hoaxes involve people who manufacture the incident to draw people's attention to the problems of ethnoviolence in their community.

The Extent of Ethnoviolence in the United States

Estimates by the Prejudice Institute (and its predecessor, the National Institute Against Prejudice and Violence) derive from rigorous case studies of cities, workplaces, and college campuses all involving sample surveys using, at different times, self-administering questionnaires, telephone interviews, and direct, face-to-face interviews. The preponderance of evidence indicates an incidence between 20 to 25 percent. This means that one out of every four or five "minority" adult Americans is harassed, intimidated, insulted, or assaulted for reasons of prejudice during the course of a year. There are variations by target group (black, white, Jewish, gay, and so on), by the locale of an incident (city, county, neighborhood), and by the specific site (school, residence, workplace). Attacks based on skin color or race are in the majority.

This is what I think we know. I qualify this because my summary is based to a large extent on my reading of research reports that were not always directly comparable. I am combining insights from studies which dealt strictly with crimes and those which more broadly studied ethnoviolence.

Race (skin color) is the major target of ethnoviolence. Gender (female) is the second most frequent, while white males are the least targeted. Who gets victimized in any given community or institutional setting seems to be determined by the stratification structure. Those towards the top are less frequently victimized than those towards the bottom.

Verbal aggression is the most frequent form of ethnoviolence. This includes face-to-face encounters (insults and name calling) as well as graffiti, leaflets, mail, e-mail, and telephone harassment.

Most ethnoviolent acts are not reported. Although variations exist across case studies, the range of variation is small. Our lowest estimate is that three-quarters of all incidents are not reported to any relevant authorities. The two most frequent reasons given for not reporting are that officials would not have done anything and there was nothing that officials could have done. Other major reasons include the denial of the significance of the incident, the rationalization that the perpetrator didn't understand what he was doing, and that this sort of thing happens all the time and so it would be of no use to report it.

According to the FBI, the incidence of hate crimes appears to be independent of the trends and distributions observed in the general crime rate. (This strongly suggests the inadequacy of a criminological model.) Unlike other antisocial phenomena such as suicide and homicide, the incidence of hate crimes also seems to be independent of economic conditions in the society.[4] At a macrosociological level, the single most consistent indicator of ethnoviolence and group conflict is the visible and rapid change of a racial/ethnic population.[5]

Trend Lines

There seem to be three trends regarding the number and character of ethnoviolent acts. First, the number of ethnoviolent events as well as

FBI-enumerated hate crimes seems to have leveled off. The period of rapid increase was from the mid-1980s to the mid-1990s. While this data suggests a plateau, state and city reports continue to show that some counties and neighborhoods are experiencing an increase in hate crimes. Second, in the earlier period, vandalism and crimes against property appeared to be the most frequent acts. However, by the mid-1990s, acts directly against people appeared to be the most frequent. (This can be seen in FBI annual reports on hate crimes as well as in reports of most states with reporting systems.[6] Maryland and Pennsylvania are good examples.) Third, as urban demographics change, intergroup dynamics are changing. Interminority ethnoviolence appears to be increasing, especially in neighborhoods or in bordering neighborhoods in which the ethnic composition is visibly changing.[7]

PERPETRATORS OF ETHNOVIOLENCE

Based on the characteristics of perpetrators of hate crimes who were apprehended usually in street or residential incidents, early researchers pointed to white teenaged boys as the major perpetrators. The notoriety of skinheads at that time doubtless contributed to that belief. This was a serious error committed because of a narrow focus on crimes, on kids who got caught, perhaps on a built-in bias against teens, and on an unwillingness to look at the ethnoviolence studies that had demonstrated clear age progressions among offenders in high schools, on college campuses, and in the workplace.

Depending on the target, location, and type of incident, somewhere between 50 and 85 percent of perpetrators are unknown. (In institutional settings such as a workplace, maybe half of the perpetrators are unknown, while in street incidents, perhaps as many as 85 percent are unknown.) By their nature, many incidents do not involve personal contact with a victim. In many incidents that do involve personal contact, victims do not know their assailant but may be able to identify a few crude demographic characteristics. Most perpetrators are male and appear to act in small groups, that is, with social support.

Ed Dunbar, a clinical psychologist, examined the court records and psychological profiles of fifty-eight persons convicted of hate crimes in Los Angeles. (This was the entire population of known and convicted offenders during the period, 1995–1997. As an aside, this was only 3.2 percent of the total reported hate crimes in which there was a known perpetrator.) Their mean age was twenty-four, and 87 percent had prior criminal convictions, 60 percent had one or more conviction for a violent offense, 59 percent had a history of substance abuse, and 22 percent had a history of psychiatric treatment. This group did not have a record of prior hate crimes, were not members of hate groups, did not articulate a racist ideology, and did not symbolically represent supremacist beliefs in their physical dress, literature or other iconography.[8]

Donald Green and his associates also found that hate crimes perpetrators, in a small sample drawn in North Carolina, did not seem to have a well-developed ideological position. Comparing the perpetrators to a sample of white supremacist group members, the researchers found that the two groups held many beliefs in common but the perpetrators were less ideologically developed, less likely to perceive a racial threat, and less likely to be concerned with organizing to defend themselves.[9]

In a study of campus ethnoviolence, we were able to identify twenty-eight student perpetrators. Although the perpetrators tended to be younger and less experienced in intergroup settings, what distinguished them from their peers was their perception of the campus as a relatively violent intergroup arena and one in which they had themselves been victimized.[10]

Types of Perpetrators

Numerous attempts have been made to develop categories of ethnoviolent actors.[11] The categories are useful in that they have implications for the understanding and treatment of perpetrators as well as the likelihood of rehabilitating them. Following are four categories I developed earlier, plus two more that have been suggested by current research.

I suggest that we first consider conceptualizing ethnoviolent actions into those that are expressive and those that are instrumental. Expressive acts are committed for thrills. These are acts of *recreational violence;* the targets tend to be opportunistic and the perpetrators seem to be operating in small groups out for kicks.

An instrumental act is a means to some end. It is generally a *responsive* act to a sense of threat to a person's status, territory, or central beliefs. (Responsive acts may be based on realistic or unrealistic perceptions. For example, they can be responses to a perceived threat that was genuine or a perceived threat that had no grounding in fact. Regardless of grounding, the instrumental actor has only a limited repertory of behaviors, and a violent response is typical.)

The third category consists of those acts motivated by an *ideological* commitment: Some categories of people are conceptualized as a nonperson or enemy.

Finally, for some, engaging in an ethnoviolent act is a means to some end unrelated to group prejudice. I call it a *collateral response*. Typically such acts involve people who are acting to maintain their position in a group, that is, to gain or retain peer acceptance.

To these four—recreational, responsive, ideological, and collateral—we may need to add two categories, one psychological and one sociological. Dunbar's work strongly suggests that we may want to consider a category of antisocial, psychopathological offenders whose life experiences make them poor risks for rehabilitative efforts. At the other extreme, it may be useful to conceptualize the "street gang" member as a particular type.

Umemoto and Mikami mapped 1,837 reported bias incidents in Los Angeles during 1994–1997 as well as engaged in observation in selected neighborhoods. Their maps indicated clusters where hate crimes occurred in relatively high density. Describing their findings, they wrote:

> While previous research has shown that hate crimes are usually perpetrated by individuals who are not members of organized hate groups, this preliminary study suggests we may find more frequent membership of perpetrators in gangs *where hate crimes cluster*. Related to this, there is strong evidence of race-bias hate crime among racial minority group-based gangs in which the major motive is not the defense of territorial boundaries against other gangs, but hatred towards a group defined by racial identification.

While gang member behavior may require conformity as a means of self-protection and membership, Umemoto and Mikami are describing a situation in which the gang has become an ideological group as well. Whether behavior in this setting is different from the behavior of hate groups remains to be discovered. However, the neighborhood base of operation creates a different dynamic from traditional hate group behavior. Where hate crimes cluster, not only do gang members display more hate crime acts, but there may be a synergistic effect that leads to an increasing level of conflict.

THE TRAUMA OF VICTIMIZATION

The politics of victimization are straightforward: victims are generally ignored. Occasionally there are "worthy" victims, that is, persons whose victimization helps forward an elite agenda. For example, when four white youths in a small South Dakota town beat to death a young American Indian, Robert Many Horses, it was not called a hate crime nor was much attention given to it. A few weeks later, when three Indian teenagers assaulted and injured a young white man, Brad Young, it became a hate crime and garnered national publicity. South Dakota Governor William Janklow released a statement deploring Young's beating but never mentioned the death of Many Horses.[12] The incident exacerbated group tensions and reaffirmed the desire of the elites for greater social control of Indian life.

Occasionally, an act of victimization is so grotesque that the national news media can transform it into a media spectacle—the Rodney King beating or the Amadou Diallo shooting. These spectacles may help the victim or his survivors achieve some equity, but their underlying function is to reaffirm the racial/ethnic status quo.

Research on ethnoviolent victimization includes several well-confirmed findings. The pivotal finding, replicated across studies, is that people who were physically or psychologically assaulted for reasons of prejudice are more traumatized than those who were victims of other sorts of similar incidents or crimes. Among the most frequent stress responses are anger, thinking about the incident over and over, nervousness, fear, social withdrawal, and revenge fantasies. Many victims reported difficulties in relations with family, friends, and significant others. Considerable numbers developed problems sleeping, eating, and with the use of alcohol and drugs. About one out of three student victims reported problems in fulfilling their studies and course work. Workplace victims experienced substantially more stress, with more than half saying that their job performance had been affected. In the workplace, victims are more likely to know their perpetrator, there is typically more than a single assailant, and in 55 percent of the instances a perpetrator was identified as a supervisor or manager.

Two additional findings in the victimization research we conducted are worthy of note. First, we have not found specific victim characteristics, or specific acts, that are predictive of the degree of trauma an ethnoviolence victim experiences. The act is surely not irrelevant, but its effect is interwoven with the past experiences and personality of the victim, the status and power of the perpetrator, and the social context in which the act occurs. (This has strong implications for victim assistance providers and other who need to avoid projecting their own definition of the situation into their assessment of trauma.)

Second, we have been seriously engaged in measuring the traumatic impact of acts of verbal aggression. Our research did confirm that verbal aggression is highly traumatic—and more so when there is a clear prejudice motivation. Further, indirect forms of verbal aggression, which we call group defamation, are almost as traumatic as personally directed ethnoviolence. These indirect forms are verbal, written, or symbolic statements that are not directed individually at the respondent but are statements about the "group" to which an individual belongs or is identified with. Examples include a spray-painted "KKK" or "Hitler was right" slogan or a racist leaflet.

Gregory Herek and his associates have studied the impact of victimization on lesbians and gay men. In their extensive survey involving over twenty-two hundred respondents in the Sacramento, California area, they reported:

> Recent hate-crime victimization appears to be associated with greater psychological distress for gay men and lesbians than is victimization in a recent nonbias crime. Lesbians and gay men who experienced an assault or other personal crime based on their sexual orientation within the previous five years reported significantly more symptoms of depression, traumatic stress, anxiety, and anger than did their counterparts (who experienced nonbias personal crimes in that period or no crimes at all).[13]

The findings clearly replicate and extend our knowledge. However, much more work, especially on the cumulative effects of ethnoviolent victimization is needed.

COVICTIMIZATION

The term *covictimization* refers to the direct or indirect witnessing of an incident of ethnoviolence in which the victim shares the same identity as the witness. We consider a physically present observer as a direct witness.

In contrast, hearing about the incident or viewing it on television is considered to be indirect witnessing. One of the great ironies of ethnoviolence and hate crimes research is the scant study given to covictimization. Workers in this area claim that the hallmark of a hate crime is that it affects the entire community, and because its impact goes beyond the immediate victim it must be treated as a separate class of crime. Moreover, the standard argument continues, because of its impact on the community, such crimes should receive an enhanced penalty. (Proponents argue that enhanced penalties are meant primarily to express community disapproval.)

What do we know about covictimization? The answer is very little. Covictims, and I say this anecdotally, appear to be less strongly affected than their victimized counterparts, but they have not escaped all consequences. Further, I have spoken with some covictims whose responses match the intensity of direct victims. There is a sense in which we are all covictims, though that sensibility is manifestly an issue of conscience and social justice. However, in the narrow sense of witnessing an ethnoviolent incident that could have as likely happened to you as to the actual victim, we have little hard data.

SUMMARY

Given the short time in which we have been studying ethnoviolent acts, including those that are legally defined as hate crimes, we have made considerable progress. However, we need to get by some barriers.

First, we can not allow the field to become confused by legal and political definitions of the problems and variables of study. Legal and judicial problems, law enforcement, and the collection of criminal statistics are genuine issues of sociological study, but they are not the central concerns of ethnoviolence research.

Second, we need to acknowledge that we are dealing with violent behavior. Not all criminal acts are violent and neither are all acts of group discrimination. However, all ethnoviolent acts are, by definition, violent. For many people, violence is narrowly construed to refer to the use of physical force. I think that is conceptually misleading; its long history in the dualistic theories of mind and body makes for a great resistance to the idea of psychological injury and trauma. Words do wound and the wounds often take longer to heal than those on the surface of our body.

There are many questions. How is violence learned? How does it become part of a person's everyday behavioral repertoire? Under what conditions is violence acceptable? When does it become normative?

I propose that violence becomes acceptable when the other person is objectified or depersonalized, and that this occurs through the act of discrimination. My guiding hypothesis is that discrimination is a necessary condition of violence, and we will not fully comprehend ethnoviolence without placing it in the context of a theory of prejudice and intergroup relations.

I believe that *objectification*—treating a person as a means to an end, as an object of little personal consequence—is central to gender violence and sexual harassment. *Depersonalization*—treating someone as a nonperson, as if they were invisible—is central to racial-based violence. At a sociological level, we know in detail how institutional and structural discrimination works. At a social psychological level, we have not yet built our analysis.

Social scientists need to keep sight of what our goals are, and I regret that we lack consensus. It is the obligation of the social scientist to help formulate a vision of a good society. The function of research is to test the degree to which the social processes of this society operate in a manner consistent with that vision as well as to confirm or disconfirm hypotheses about social alternatives. Through the study of prejudice, ethnoviolence, and the dimensions of intergroup relations, we should be able to formulate propositions about the nature of an egalitarian society.

NOTES

1. Andrew Sullivan, "What's So Bad about Hate?" *New York Times Magazine*, 26 September 1999.

2. Donileen R. Loseke, *Thinking about Social Problems* (New York: Aldine De Gruyter, 1999), 25.

3. Sullivan, "What's So Bad about Hate?"

4. Donald P. Green, Jack Glaser, and Andrew Rich, "From Lynching to Gay Bashing: The Elusive Connection Between Economic Conditions and Hate Crimes," *Journal of Personality and Social Psychology* 75 (1998), 1–11.

5. Robin Williams, "Reduction of Intergroup Tensions," Social Science Research Council, 1948; Howard J. Ehrlich, *The Social Psychology of Prejudice* (New

York: Wiley, 1973); Karen Umemoto and C. Kimi Mikami, "A Profile of Race-Bias Hate Crimes in Los Angeles County," *Western Criminology Review* 2.2 (1999).

6. Bureau of Justice Statistics, "A Policymaker's Guide to Hate Crimes," Washington, DC, 1997.

7. Umemoto and Mikami.

8. Edward Dunbar, "Towards a Profile of Violent Hate Criminals: Aggressive, Situational, and Ideological Signifiers of Bias Motivated Offenders," paper presented to the UCLA/SPSSI Conference on Hate Crimes, 29 October 1999.

9. Donald P. Green, Jack Glaser, and Andrew Rich, "From Lynching to Gay Bashing: The Elusive Connection Between Economic Conditions and Hate Crime," *Journal of Personality and Social Psychology* 75 (1998), 82–92.

10. Howard J. Ehrlich, Fred Pincus, and Deborah Lacy, http://www.research .umbc.edu/~pincus, 1977.

11. Gregory Herek and Kevin Berrill, eds., *Hate Crimes* (Thousand Oaks, CA: Sage, 1992); Jack McDevitt and Jack Levin, *Hate Crimes* (New York: Plenum Press, 1993).

12. *St. Paul Pioneer Press*, 28 August 1999.

13. Gregory M. Herek, J. Roy Gillis, and Jeanine C. Cogan, "Psychological Sequelae of Hate-Crime Victimization Among Lesbian, Gay, and Bisexual Adults," *Journal of Consulting and Clinical Psychology* 67.6 (1999), 945–951.

3

FURTHER OBSERVATIONS
Some Questions, Some Answers

The lack of an articulated theory regarding prejudice, discrimination, and conflict is the key deficit in the study of ethnoviolence and hate crimes. Additionally, the literature grossly misconstrues prejudice, leading too often to assertions that are false by definition or have been invalidated by past research. One may rarely find any discussion of the correlation between discrimination and ethnoviolence, when conceptually, if not empirically, discrimination should be construed as a necessary condition of ethnoviolence. That construction might lead to an entirely different approach to analysis and intervention.

Analysts often confuse a crime with a sociological concept, thus missing the full range of the phenomenon. Because of this confusion, they focus on issues of law enforcement unique to the identification of hate crimes and the development of hate crimes jurisprudence. Moreover, hate speech, which is a primary signifier of a hate crime, is often passed over as if it were an insignificant event.

Premised on the belief that hate crimes and acts of ethnoviolence are about issues of power—the ability of a dominant group to maintain its dominance through physical and psychological mechanisms of oppression—this chapter explores the concepts of ethnoviolence and hate crimes and offers a reinterpretation.

STRUGGLING FOR DEFINITION

The Hate Crime Statistics Act of 1990 precipitated many of the difficulties facing jurists and social scientists today because it does not clearly define a hate crime or identify how you can enumerate such occurrences.

Three consequences have followed the application of the concept of hate crimes and the laws concerning them. First is the matter of who is covered by these laws. This question has been largely answered by the courts, as statutes of varying breadth and ambiguity have been tested since 1990. In American courts, a crime is recorded as a hate crime because of the group membership of the victim. Most statues also refer to the intent of the perpetrator to intimidate or harass someone because of his or her group membership.[1]

While there may be little ambiguity in limiting the concept and the law of hate crimes to major crimes against persons or property, the definitional issue remains. That is, there is still a dispute regarding which groups are eligible to be included as potential victims and what acts should be covered by legislation.[2]

A second consequence, clearly unintended and largely unrecognized, is the opportunity presented to ultraconservative and right-wing critics who have been able to use the ambiguities and errors of hate crime regulations and laws to ridicule and discredit civil rights and left liberal legislative interventions. The central conservative argument appears to be that most events labeled "hate crimes" are minor, infrequent incidents that do not warrant special attention, and that singling them out is an attempt by liberals to regulate speech and punish people for what they think.

The third consequence is the misapplication of a political label to a social science concept. The concept of a hate crime has been in a protracted state of definition and redefinition that it is, at best, a sensitizing concept, lacking rigor nominally and operationally. Without consensus on a reasonable conception of a hate crime—or, more appropriately, with an absence of agreement on whether a crime was entailed and whether that crime was motivated by hate—the findings of much current research and scholarship rest on a methodologically insecure base.

Developments in the United Kingdom parallel those in the United States. Beginning with the 1965 Race Relations Act, the legislative focus was on the intent of the actor. In the UK's 1998 Crime and Disorder Act, concern was more specifically focused on the "hostile motivation" of the offender based on the victim's real or perceived membership in a racial group.[3]

CONCEPTUALIZING ETHNOVIOLENCE

In 1993, two books were published that together signaled what was to be a central controversy in the field of ethnoviolence. The more popular of the two works is Jack Levin and Jack McDevitt's *Hate Crimes,* which bears the lurid subtitle "The Rising Tide of Bigotry and Bloodshed." The book contains no reference to prejudice, racism, or discrimination. It pays almost no attention to victims and their trauma. Instead, references to the police and the law enforcement–judicial system are central. Conversely, the other book, Milton Kleg's *Hate Prejudice and Racism,* contains no significant references to the police or justice system. Rather, it focuses on prejudice and discrimination and devotes two chapters to the ameliorative effects of education. Both books allocate considerable space to hate groups. The fundamental division between researchers in the field is clear in these contrasting works: a focus on law and the criminal justice system versus a focus on prejudice and discrimination. Most noteworthy is that neither book gives serious attention to the structure of intergroup relations.

A chasm exists between criminologists and jurists on one side and social scientists on the other. The law enforcement side is focused on control, punishment, deterrence, and incarceration. Social scientists focus on developing an understanding and theory of intergroup relations. Both sides often lay claim to a concern with alleviating group tensions. Many of us, including myself, see our role as action researcher and, in that capacity, try to move between community activism and social research, applying what we know as activists to our research and what we know as researchers to our activism.

I introduced the term *ethnoviolence* in 1986, in part to emphasize the misleading character of the concept of hate crimes but also to question the adoption of the compromised notion of *bias crimes* and *bias incidents.* The use of *bias* hides the target of the act. Further, construing the event as an *incident* is far too antiseptic. Politically, these neologisms function to downgrade the social significance of the issue.

Ethnoviolence refers to violence motivated by group prejudice. Defining violence, however, is a formidable task. The *Oxford English Dictionary* devotes six pages to its exposition, and the *Penguin Dictionary of Sociology* does not include *violence* as a sociological term. It is, after all, a term of the natural language and not a technical concept within some theory. At its core is the sense of actions that are intense, usually strong in feeling or expression, and characterized by doing harm or injury and attempting to intimidate or control. In short, violence is harm done to another person. Some analysts have placed violence in a more political context as any violation of a person's basic human rights. The sociologist Johann Galtung has defined a violent act as any act that prevents people from realizing their full potential.

As a society, and within the law, we tend to regard violence as a physical event. Murder, rape, and assault are considered acts of extreme violence. But what about being robbed of one's self? What about being dehumanized to the point that you are treated as an object, a nonperson? The frequency of such treatment is outstanding. In our research at the Prejudice Institute, we have observed students and workers reporting dehumanizing incidents on the average 18 to 25 percent of all experienced incidents, with a high of 53 percent, depending on the sample. The following examples are from our workplace studies.

- Sally, a black office worker, is never spoken to directly by her supervisor. Notes are left on her desk, and when one other person is present, the supervisor tells the other person, "Tell Sally that I expect these reports tomorrow."
- In the large office of an insurance company with many clerks seated at desks, new computers are distributed to everyone except the isolated black clerk. A computer is even placed on an empty desk adjacent to hers.
- For three month after she started her new job, Tomeika, the sole black employee, had no idea who to report to. "I was never even instructed how to do a time sheet. For a month and a half, no one even spoke to me. People would pass me by and not speak. I went to the director asking for work to do and to be assigned to someone. He said he couldn't do it at the time. Eventually a team leader approached me with a small amount of work to do. He really did not have the authority to do this. It paid off. I've been with him ever since."

To treat people as if they were nonpersons is to act toward them with violence. It denies their basic humanness, their psychological integrity, and their dignity as a people.

The most frequent class of incidents is verbal aggression. This is true in the community, at workplaces, and on college campuses. These are seldom crimes, but they are acts of ethnoviolence. As everyday events, they are critical to an understanding of intergroup relations, the trauma experienced by those victimized, and our ability to intervene effectively.

In the United States, the legal basis for a response to verbal and symbolic assaults, typically labeled "hate speech," is still fermenting. Great Britain, France, and Germany, among other European nations, seem less hesitant to respond legally to insults, name calling, ethnophaulisms, and the displays of socially recognized symbols of prejudice and racism. Nevertheless, the *effects* of hate speech have not been dealt with as directly as ethnoviolence or hate crimes. In my conception, words wound; thus, hate speech is a violent act.

U.S. jurisprudence has permitted a distinction between *speech* and *conduct*, but this distinction has two major problems. The first is the implication that words are not a form of behavior, or at least not a form of behavior that can be subject to regulation in the context of race/ethnic relations. This is based on a serious misunderstanding of psychology. Whether we want to point to the clinical writings of Sigmund Freud, the social psychology of Charles Horton Cooley, the philosophical writings of George Herbert Mead and Ernst Cassirer, or the anthropology of Benjamin Whorf, a long history in the social sciences—going back a century—emphasizes the critical importance of symbolization and verbal behavior in human interaction.

The second implication is that the refusal to consider insulting, contemptuous, humiliating speech in this context is a political decision. Speech with an underlying motivation of prejudice is a major mechanism of social control. Protecting such speech is mainly the work of dominant, white, European American jurists.

Can anyone doubt the force of such slogans as "Hitler was right" or the display of such symbols as a noose? Of course, not all words and symbols are equal in their virulence, and their meaning changes by speaker, by target, and by time and place. How this operates is an empirical question for sociology and not something to be decided by political fiat.

We do, however, have some substantial empirical evidence. I assume that we define acts as violent on the basis of two criteria: One, the act violates important norms of society and frequently does so at unexpected times and places; and two, the act creates considerable harm to the victim. It is this important second point that is our focus. In our studies at the Prejudice Institute, we developed a checklist to measure the consequences of various forms of victimization. Using face-to-face interviews, phone interviews, and self-administered questionnaires, we asked respondents to indicate whether they had experienced any of nineteen psychophysiological symptoms of post-traumatic stress as a consequence of the ethnoviolence they had experienced.

In approximately three thousand cases, we found that victims of physical violence or threats of physical violence motivated by prejudice experienced almost as many symptoms as victims of violence not motivated by prejudice. Our control group of nonvictims experienced the fewest symptoms. Our data does not permit us to make any inference as to the degree of incapacity of the victim nor the length of time these stressful behaviors persisted. However, McDevitt's data from the Boston Police Department shows that victims of ethnoviolent assault are beaten more seriously and hospitalized longer than other assault victims.[4] An additional finding in our studies further bolsters our argument for the inclusion of verbal violence in our conceptualization of prejudice-motivated violence. These are acts of verbal violence directed not at a specific individual but at a racial/ethnic category—what I call group defamation. Here are some examples from our campus studies.

- Members of a fraternity dressed in and distributed T-shirts bearing the slogan, "Club Faggots, Not Seals."
- A campus newspaper printed a cartoon depicting a Chanukah menorah with missiles instead of candles, with the caption, "We wish you a Happy Holocaust."
- A cross was burned in front of the administration building at a small, mainly black college.

None of these acts were directed at a single other, and most of the students, staff, and faculty on these campuses probably only heard about these incidents as opposed to directly observing them. There is no doubt that these acts were insulting and threatening. What is material here is that our data indicates that these acts of group insult induce significant stress. The trauma associated with this form of ethnoviolence may not be as great as in a face-to-face encounter, but it should not be ignored. A shove or a finger in the ribs, which legally qualifies as a simple assault and thus as a hate crime, is unlikely to invoke any greater trauma than a "Happy Holocaust" card.

Researchers in this area need to remind themselves that the trauma experienced by a person in response to ethnoviolence is not mechanistically determined. Rather, it is an emergent based on the victim's biography and personality, the history and visibility of the act, the act itself, its perceived consequences, and the characteristics of the perpetrator. In sum, it is often difficult to predict the response of a victim based only on the knowledge of the prejudice-motivated act.

MORE ON THE PERPETRATORS

Are those who perpetrate violent acts motivated by prejudice different from those whose violence was not motivated by prejudice? Do those who employ verbal and psychological acts of violence and ethnoviolence differ in some significant manner from those who employ physical acts of violence? We don't know the answers to these questions, but we need to address them if we want to understand prejudice-motivated behavior. At present, the research evidence leads us to answer that some differences exist among these different actors. However, the differences do not appear to be categorical (that is, either-or differences) and the problem might be better conceptualized by constructing a typology or profile.

From a methodological standpoint, perpetrators are hard to find, and those that we do find may not be representative of the larger class of offenders. For example, we may observe a considerable number of male teenage perpetrators, but only because they are more likely than adults to get caught. Further, in some instances, prejudice may be a weak component of an actor's behavior, and in other instances the offender's articulation of a motive may come later as a rationalization after the ethnoviolent act itself.

We raise questions about the characteristics of perpetrators for two key reasons. The most obvious is that if the identification of an act is in error, generalizations about perpetrators will be in error. Second, we need to understand perpetrators because we are concerned with intervention. By *intervention* I mean both the ability to take preventative measures and the ability to develop rehabilitative programs. From the standpoint of a clinician, this is an appropriate concern. From a sociological standpoint, however, the pursuit of a perpetrator syndrome or typology may inadvertently lead us down a reductionist path. Ethnoviolence occurs in a sociocultural setting, a setting into which the perpetrators were socialized and in which they live.

NOTES

1. A concise summary of the legal history of U.S. hate crime legislation can be found in Ryken Gratett and Valerie Jenness, "The Birth and Maturation of Hate Crime Policy in the United States," *American Behavioral Scientist* 45 (2001), 668–696.

2. Consider this case: In 2001, the resident cat of the public library in Escondido, California, attacked the assistance dog of Richard R. Espinosa (whose disability is a panic disorder), inflicting cuts that so discomforted Espinosa that he filed a $1.5 million lawsuit against the library for the "terror, humiliation, shame, embarrassment, mortification, chagrin, depression, panic, anxiety, flashbacks, [and] nightmares" the dog's injuries caused him. In April 2002, Espinosa amended his complaint, claiming that his disability puts him and his dog into a specially protected class and thus the cat's actions should be considered a "hate crime" (MSNBC.com, 5 April, 2002).

3. For a comparison of British and American laws, see Frederick M. Lawrence, "Bias Crime in a Multi-Cultural Society," Boston University School of Law Working Paper Series, http://www.bu.edu/law/faculty/papers, 2000.

4. Jack Levin and Jack McDevitt, *Hate Crimes: The Rising Tide of Bigotry and Bloodshed* (New York: Plenum Press, 1993).

PART II

THE NEWS MEDIA

4

ETHNOVIOLENCE AND THE NEWS MEDIA

The news media appears to be people's main source of information about current events. Two out of three Americans claim to follow current events regularly.[1] A November 2001 *ABC* poll found that almost half of all Americans over eighteen indicate that they get some of their news from the Internet.

At the same time, recent studies reveal that fewer young people read the newspaper. Richard Morin, as polling editor for the *Washington Post*, argued that young people today are less knowledgeable of politics than twenty-five years ago. A 2000 Pew Poll found that more than one-third of a national sample of persons under thirty got their news primarily from late-night comedians.

Studies have shown that the news media is a primary source for the learning and maintenance of ethnic attitudes and the justification of many forms of discrimination. As is the case for all social processes, the details are inordinately complex and change with the social position and theoretical stance of the observer. A good example is the differential perceptions of the news media by black and white audiences. While 30 percent of black Americans believe that the news media treat people of all races equally, 76 percent of whites believe that equal treatment is the case.[2]

In this chapter I present a theoretical model for understanding this social process. I call it the *media-environment model*. Here, I will present the basic features of the model.

THE MEDIA-ENVIRONMENT MODEL

Developed from the theoretical perspective of symbolic interaction, the media-environment model is built on George Gerbner's cultural ecology model and the media criticism of Neil Postman and Noam Chomsky. The primary focus of this model is sociological: Its central concern is how the media functions to maintain the subordinate status of minorities, deviants, and dissidents. Although its focus is on newspaper and television news, my comments are applicable in large measure to the entertainment media as well. Following are the basic principles of the model in brief.

The first principle is that within industrialized countries, no mass media–free environments exist. The second principle is that media effects are cumulative. It is not that a single video game is violent nor that one newscast overflows with stories of crimes and disasters. The issue is that people are repeatedly exposed to them. The best metaphor for this cumulative exposure might be that of a toxin: Most people are affected and experience a chronic reaction, although some develop a relative immunity.

The third principle of the media-environment model is that the news and entertainment media are conceptualized as agents of socialization. As such, their function is to communicate the dominant values of society. They do so by

- the continual display of traditional authority structures, the result of which is to increase people's dependency on legitimate authority as well as reaffirming the necessity of authority;
- legitimating the American way of life, upholding and glorifying American social institutions;
- presenting a world view that recapitulates the stratification structure of society through gender, racial, and ethnic stereotyping;
- depressing public consciousness of class, inequality, and power;
- placating political dissent and depicting the dissenter as an antimodel
- making the political personal and transforming the social to the psychological;
- routinizing violence through its everyday appearance in the news media, leading people to construe violence as inescapable and, therefore, socially acceptable;
- providing the illusion of a social order built on a value consensus.

As the research of George Gerbner has shown, the consequence of these mechanisms of socialization is to foster the perception that the world is a mean and dangerous place. This perception enables the political elites to achieve the public acceptance of increased social controls (through state-sanctioned propaganda, legislation, and the deployment of additional control agents).

CASE STUDIES AND APPLICATIONS

Most editors and corporate managers of the news media have appointed themselves as guardians, or gatekeepers, of democracy in America. They have developed a script for covering minorities and the movements of social change and civil resistance. The script has four components and is invoked in defense of the status quo.

The first component is that those dissatisfied with the status quo (especially if engaged in public protest) are not nice people. They are extremists, leftists, and anarchists. They are poorly informed and do not represent the larger population. Although small in numbers, protesters endanger the good order of society. Following the post 9/11 government propaganda, a new entry to the script equates protest with terrorism and a threat to national security.

The second component is that protestors are undemocratic, attempting to impose their will on the majority. They are typically "reverse racists." Third, minorities protesting for social justice are typically hypersensitive; their concerns are misplaced. The fourth component is that divisiveness in society is the result of protest itself.

These four propositions make up a frame. A *media frame* is an organizing principle in which the news media selects a single component and through selection, emphasis, and exclusion make that stand for the entire picture.

A standard technique for maintaining the state of intergroup relations is to deny the existence of conflict. The treatment of this poll is a classic example where the positive results are cast in a frame that excludes negative results. Here are two headlines describing the same Gallup poll (8 August 1988):

"Poll: Many Feel Racism Abating" (*Baltimore Evening Sun*)
"Poll Finds Majority Believe Race Prejudice Is Still Strong" (*New York Times*)

It is hard to believe that they cover the same poll. The *Sun* headline writer found the only positive finding in an otherwise negative set of results and moved two paragraphs to the lead, writing a headline that fit that single finding. This act becomes understandable when you learn that at the time, the *Sun* was in a state of denial regarding ethnoviolence in the city.

Another facet of denial is the denial of persistent, chronic social pathology. Poverty, prisons, deteriorating schools, and homelessness are part of everyday life. As such, they are not newsworthy events. However, a prison riot or a homeless person set afire by a gang is a spectacle, and as such is deemed newsworthy. Related to the issues of protest and denial are anger and rage. In the coverage of protests, particularly prison "riots," strikes, and the protests of local community groups, the news media focus on the anger expressed by those not in power. This focus distracts people from the real issues—that is, the causes of this anger—and depicts the protestors as malcontents, perhaps scary and out-of-control.

Imagine this scene: a strike of hospital workers. The issue is overtime pay and working hours. The camera pans on a shop steward, a black male who is so enraged that he is barely comprehensible. The strike had been settled, or so he thought, and the union was preparing the membership to go back to work when hospital administrators, having second thoughts, withdrew their settlement offering. He is screaming about bad faith and details of the settlement that simply make no sense to the TV audience. The next shot is of a white male doctor in a long white coat standing in front of a bookcase. In soft, well-modulated tones he begins, "I don't know what these people want. We agreed to all their conditions."

So who do you believe: the fuming, inarticulate black hospital worker or the doctor, a voice of beneficent white authority?

The fragmentation of news, which is reporting events without a context or without a conclusion, is ultimately confusing and sometimes depressing. For example, on 18 January 1998, Patrick Purdy entered an elementary schoolyard in Stockton, California, and fired one hundred rounds at the students, most of whom were the children of Southeast Asian refugees. Five were killed, and twenty-nine children and one teacher were wounded. Newspapers across the country gave the story front-page coverage. And, as is typical, the story disappeared in a few days. The perpetrator, who killed himself afterwards, was presumably a man gone mad. Almost one year later, the California Attorney General's office issued a statement. Their investigation indicated that Purdy had harbored extreme prejudice against Vietnamese, and that what seemed like a random crime by a sick man was, in fact, a spectacular hate crime. This conclusion to what was once front-page news was reported by only a handful of papers. Emblematic of the coverage was a one-column story in the *Washington Post*. This fragmentation of the story— a madman's violent act or a major hate crime—was created by applying the wrong frame and allowing it to stand.

Here's a different form of fragmentation. On November 18, 2002, the *Associated Press* sent out a story featuring the attempt of Democrats to block the appointment of Dennis Shedd to the Fourth Circuit Court of Appeals in Richmond, Virginia. The only reason for their action presented in the news report was that "he has been insensitive in civil rights and employment discrimination cases." The storyline was clear. The Democrats had again blocked a judicial appointment by the president. But the other parts of the story were missing: there was no explanation of "insensitivity" or any acknowledgment that 90 percent of the president's judicial appointments had not been blocked.

Fragmented stories are the stuff of TV news. According to the *Project for Excellence in Journalism*, fifteen-to thirty-second stories are common, with seven out of ten stories one minute or shorter (February 2000). The Prejudice Institute's twelve-city study displays an average of sixteen stories in fourteen minutes (see Chapter 7). Fragmentation, the reporting of events incompletely without context or without an ending, is confusing. Even the careful reader and viewer become unable to decipher the real stories or establish a full understanding of discrete events.

One reason for this is that not all victims of ethnoviolence, or for that matter most forms of victimization, are covered by the news media. To gain coverage, they have to be "worthy victims." (I expropriate this term from Noam Chomsky and Edward Herman, who used it more in a context of international news coverage). Victims are "worthy" only if their victimization can be used by the gatekeepers of news to fit their agenda. For example, the people who died in the twin towers of the World Trade Center on 9/11 were worthy, whereas the people in Afghanistan who died in revenge were unworthy. How many Iraqi civilians died as a result of the war? The news media and the Army don't count them. The latest, best estimates are highly variable. At the end of 2006 it was likely that 600,000 civilians had died; almost half were children less than fifteen years old. Manifestly, they are not worthy victims. (A summary of the various estimates appears in the *Guardian*, 19 March 2008, by Jonathan Steele and Suzanne Goldenberg.)

My prototypical worthy victim is O. J. Simpson. As a handsome, black, well-spoken, wealthy football star, Simpson almost escaped the symbolic of worthiness. The problem was that he was too light-skinned. Maybe if he were darker, he could be hated a little more. So what happened? On 27 June 1994, both *Time* magazine and *Newsweek* put him on the cover, running his full-face police mug shot. *Newsweek* ran the original, but *Time*'s cover was digitally manipulated so that his face was darker, unshaven, and blurrier. Now, as a dark-skinned, unkempt man, he was worthy of the charges against him. As for his dead wife, Nicole Brown Simpson, in a single shot in a bikini, she was a worthy victim. But show her with her racially integrated family, and she became unworthy.

The headline "Korean Grocer Killed" is more subtle. Presumably, the ethnicity of the victim had no necessary relation to the story. The headline, however, appeared in the *Evening Sun* at a time of intense Korean-black conflict in Baltimore with many incidents involving Korean shopkeepers in black neighborhoods. Although the reporter did not know the ethnicity of the assailant, the headline writer's insensitivity led many readers to assume that the perpetrator was black and that this was another incident of group conflict. As it turned out, the killer was Korean.

The victims of society are often black. The distortion of images based on current stereotypes is rampant. For example, in 2000, while 29 percent of the poor in the United States were black, 62 percent of those portrayed in *Time* and *Newsweek*'s photographs of the poor were black. On network evening newscasts, the comparable figure was 65 percent. The same distortion appears on the news regarding the percentage of blacks that are suspects in crime stories.

The depiction and overstatement of violent crime is another form of distorting intergroup relations. This treatment of violent crime overstates both the level of violence in the community and the proportion of minorities, especially blacks and Latinos, as the perpetrators of these crimes. This is facilitated by the fact that in most studies two out of every five minutes of local TV news is dedicated to crime coverage.

During the 1990s, as the national homicide rate declined by 20 percent, its coverage on the evening news went up by a factor of 7.[3] Another perspective is that homicides account for about one-to two-tenths of 1 percent of all arrests in the United States. However, 28 percent of all crimes on the evening news are homicides. In fact, only 2 percent of people in a nationwide sample report that they were victimized by any form of violent crime in the past 12 months.[4] Victims shown are predominantly white; the suspects are predominantly black.

Another form of discrimination in the news media is in the selection of news sources, that is, the people asked to comment on or explain the news. Here the most discriminatory selections are routine and transparent. White, corporate business people or representatives of conservative, right-of-center think tanks are the most frequent sources of news and commentary. For example, in 2001, the total number of appearances by labor representatives on U.S. nightly television was thirty-one. Corporate executives appeared thirty times more often.[5] Think tank spokespersons appearing on TV were 50 percent conservative and right leaning, 30 percent centrist, and 20 percent progressive or left leaning.[6]

One study observed the guests on fourteen regularly scheduled political talk shows from 8 November 2000 to 11 December 2000, when the Supreme Court heard oral arguments in *Bush v. Gore*. There were 857 speakers in all, 95 percent of whom were white. As Deborah Mathis, author and fellow of the Harvard Shorenstein Center on the Press, Politics, and Public Policy, said: "Whom [the press] does or does not invite to speak with authority makes a statement about whose opinions are valued."[7] We approach the issue of authority in more detail in Chapter 7.

Media Tenor, an international media research group, analyzed 14,632 sources appearing on *ABC World News Tonight, NBC Nightly News,* and *CBS Evening News* in 2001. As you might expect, the U.S. sources were overwhelmingly white (92 percent) and male (81 percent). Only 7 percent were black, and no other ethnic group was represented more than 0.7 percent of the time. As you might not expect, 75 percent of the sources were Republican and 24 percent Democrat. Antiestablishment independents, such as Ralph Nader, appeared as 0.03 percent of all politicians quoted.[8]

The op-ed page of the newspaper is another selective forum often limited to the elite. Colman McCarthy, a former columnist and editorial writer for the *Washington Post*, comments that the *Post*'s op-ed page is "a bulletin board for establishment heavies whose columns read like memos shared among the good old boys." McCarthy estimates that the ratio of right-wingers and centrists to leftists is 50 to 1; 2 percent of the op-ed pieces expressed a progressive perspective.[9]

The results of a Fairness and Accuracy in Reporting (FAIR) study of syndicated columnists in mainstream papers are congruent with McCarthy's limited data. Of the major, syndicated columnists, 86 percent are white males. There are three women and four blacks, and the black columnists are centrist or conservative. Ellen Goodman and Molly Ivins represent women and the liberal left, but Ivins died in 2007.

Not only are news sources chosen selectively with regard to race/ethnicity, gender, and social position, but the content of what is reported—the news itself—is highly selective with regard to these dimensions. The absence of coverage, that is, silence, may be the most insidious form of control. Noncoverage not only distorts the past but also misdirects us in the present.

Ethnoviolence is a potent example. Any enterprising reporter can go to the police blotter or the reports to human relations commissions to find stories. For example, two researchers at Northwestern, David Protess and James S. Ettema, reviewed the records of bias crimes reported to the Chicago Commission on Human Relations and the reports in the weekly and daily newspapers for a one-year period. Their major finding: Only 9 percent of the bias crimes reported to the commission were mentioned in the press. The incidents selected for coverage were more likely to be more serious crimes. The spectacular character—or what the gatekeepers would likely call the newsworthiness of the incident—rather than the pervasiveness of ethnoviolence determined the story. Following their research model, I compared the *Sun* papers' coverage of Maryland bias crimes and incidents over a three and a half year period, from January 1990 through July 1993. I compared the reports made to the State Human Relations Commission by local police departments with its coverage in either of the two daily *Sun* papers. I found that, for every eighty-two incidents officially recorded, only one was reported in either newspaper (approximately 1.2 percent).

Since everyday ethnoviolence is generally perceived as not newsworthy, it is worth asking why it is covered at all. One reason is that the story itself can be cast as a representation of how well the "system" is working—especially if perpetrators are vilified and victims are supported. More importantly, from the standpoint of its social function, reporting ethnoviolence serves as a social reminder that group conflict persists and that the dominant group is still dominant.

A second reason is that the underlying effect of the reporting or nonreporting of prejudice, discrimination, and ethnoviolence is to reaffirm the subordinate status of women, of "traditional" minorities, and of political and cultural dissidents. This process of reaffirmation fragments and distorts the news of intergroup problems and generally alienates the underrepresented and those members of the dominant group who are genuinely civically involved.

Another category of news related to civil rights that is not covered is local government, or what is called public affairs in the media jargon. News of local public affairs is virtually absent from the airwaves. A study of forty-five TV stations in one week during October 2003 offers a dramatic example. The Alliance for Better Campaigns coded 7,560 hours of news programming and found that only 13 hours, less than one-half of 1 percent, were devoted to the news of local government.[10]

Prejudice underlies most of the mechanisms presented here. My colleague, Robert Purvis, documented an almost hidden act of stereotype assignment that he uncovered by comparing coverage in two newspapers. He exposed this in a letter he wrote to the editor of the *Evening Sun*. The letter was not answered. He wrote:

> Recently the *Evening Sun* carried a *New York Times* news service report about welfare mothers' struggle to gain employment and break free of welfare. The original report included a case study of a particular woman's struggle, coupled with substantial information about the national scope of this problem. The *Evening Sun*'s edited version served to trivialize the issue by eliminating the national perspective and focusing solely on the limited, anecdotal case study.

One pernicious piece of editing in this piece is worth mentioning. At one point the report describes the mother's inability to provide adequate day care for her children while she worked. In the original report, the mother "shrugged helplessly" in response to this dilemma. In the *Evening Sun*, she merely "shrugged." The former description conveys the mother's anguish, while the edited version equally suggests indifference. If you doubt that many of your readers will incorrectly infer the mother's indifference from your edited version, you are seriously out of touch with some of the most powerful forces at work in our society today.

CHOOSING THE NEWS

Choosing what news events or issues to cover is a political act. The choice is a reflection of social priorities. The decision may be external, such as pressure from advertisers.[11] Conversely, the decision may be internal, one of self-censorship.[12]

Some editors and corporate managers have appointed themselves guardians of democracy in America. In that capacity they regard their publication or programs as a resource for controlling information that they deem politically problematic. The wars in Afghanistan and Iraq have certainly exposed the ethnocentrism and political bias of many in the entertainment and news media. The level of control ranges from the absurd, such as a Seattle TV station declaring it would not cover demonstrations if the participants "were not behaving properly," to the jingoistic, such as the chairman of the Cable News Network ordering reporters to paint the Taliban with a decided negative tint, to the ludicrous banning of one hundred fifty selections of popular music by Clear Channel Communication, the largest radio chain in the country. The ban included such compositions as *Peace Train, What a Wonderful World, Bridge over Troubled Water*, and John Lennon's *Imagine*.

Although such transparent incidents of bias are not common, it is unusual for the major gatekeepers to openly state their position and to place it in an explicit ideological frame. Perhaps the boldest articulation of this comes from Katherine Graham, the late publisher of the *Washington Post* and *Newsweek*: "There are some things the general public does not need to know and shouldn't. I believe democracy flourishes when the government can take legitimate steps to keep its secrets and when the press can decide whether to print what it knows."[13]

NOTES

1. *Extra*, May–June 2000.

2. *Brills Content*, June 2000, 40.

3. Center for Media and Public Affairs cited by Geneva Overholzer, *Washington Post*, 24 December 1999.

4. Gallup.com, 3 December 2004.

5. *Harpers Index*, September–October, 2002.

6. *Extra* July–August, 2001.

7. *UTNE Reader,* Fall 2001, 34.

8. *Extra*, May–June 2002.

9. *The Progressive,* October 2001.

10. Cited by Bill Moyers, "Journalism under Fire," a paper presented to the Society of Professional Journalists, September 2004.

11. See, for example, Arthur E. Rowse, *Drive-By Journalism* (Monroe, ME: Common Courage Press, 2000), especially chapter 8.

12. Eric Alterman, *The Nation*, 5 June 2000, 12.

13. *Regardies* magazine, 4–10 April 1990.

5

THE GATEKEEPERS OF NEWSPAPERS

The following stories are true. Only the names and some details have been changed to protect the unwitting.

The nuclear power plant thirty miles upwind from the city served by the *Daily Planet* has had a potentially serious accident. The temperature is rising in the holding tanks for the spent fuel rods, and more portentously, there is a major radiation leakage around the seams of an original, now brittle network of piping. Sam Sapphire, a reliable and seasoned reporter, is sent to cover the story. The problem: Sam doesn't even know the difference between ionizing and nonionizing radiation and hasn't the slightest idea how a nuclear reactor works. The events, including the evacuation of neighboring towns and subsequent investigations, continue for a year. Sam's reporting is substantially ignorant and initially dependent on industry and government briefings. By the end of the year, however, he has become fairly knowledgeable and the character of his stories has changed.

Ellen Stanton is sent out to do a feature on a new organization in town—the Center Against Racial and Ethnic Violence. Ellen is a recent graduate from a prestigious journalism school and has little urban experience and virtually no intergroup experience. She has no understanding of the difference between prejudice and discrimination. (This is much like not knowing the difference between ionizing and nonionizing radiation.) Moreover, she believes prejudice is an instinctive behavior and that little can be done about it. Her story, carried as the features section lead, contains five errors of fact and concept in the lead paragraph alone. At one point, late in the story, she describes the institute director as "claiming that prejudice is learned," as if this were a point of contention.

Who gets assigned to a story is an act that can have considerable political consequence. In particular, stories about race and ethnic relations can affect the level of group tensions in a community. Such stories can play on common misconceptions and group stereotypes or focus on anger and pathology. Sam's stories unwittingly supported the industry, undermined citizens' protests, and misinformed people about matters affecting their safety and health. In contrast, Ellen's story looks like it can be written off. It did not appear to do any palpable damage (except for some apparently minor embarrassment to the reputation of the Center). In fact, her story reaffirmed many of the dominant misconceptions concerning intergroup relations using the legitimacy of her newspaper to support it. The wrong information spread by the story is part of the glue that holds together the conflictual fabric of group relations.

It is my contention that assigning a reporter who knows little about race and ethnic relations to cover a story about race and ethnic relations is a political act. It does not matter whether the reporter or editor intended a political outcome. Intergroup relations today are a power struggle. The depiction of those relations inescapably has implications for maintaining the status quo or undermining the power balance.

Most readers assume that editors attempt to select the best available reporter for a story assignment, and that in dealing with race and ethnic relations, editors select seasoned and sensitive reporters. Could you imagine someone being sent to cover professional soccer playoffs or the local college lacrosse championships who had never seen either game? It wouldn't happen. Why? Because sports are deemed to be so important that every paper has regular sports writers with regular beats. Papers have food editors, religion editors, city hall and state house beats, education beats, and local gossip beats. In the context of these specializations, the decision not to have a race and ethnic (R&E) beat should be construed as a political decision. It is a statement that implies two independent conclusions. First, intergroup relations are not an arena of community life with any special significance. Second, no particular body of knowledge concerning prejudice, discrimination, and group conflict requires specialization.

What is published and how it is framed—that is, what is minimized and what is emphasized—help determine the public political agenda. What doesn't get published can play an even more significant role because it may never make it to the public agenda. Reporting the news of race and ethnic relations has serious implications for the social capital of a community, for developing an ethos of multiculturalism, and for refining an American democratic process.

STUDY ONE: THE EDITORS

In this section, I present the outcome of interviews with the major gate-keepers of what is reported in the leading circulating newspapers in the United States. The term gatekeeper is academic journalist jargon and conventionally refers to anyone in the process of news reporting who has the legitimate authority to make decisions about what gets reported to the public. Here I focus on editors; in the second part of this chapter, I talk to the reporters.

A large newspaper has many gatekeepers: the publisher, the owner, and various editors, advertisers, and reporters are some of the more obvious. Many more stories and leads come into a daily newspaper than ever get published. Ben Bagdikian, former dean of journalism at the University of California, Berkeley, estimates in his book *The Information Machines* that in large metropolitan dailies gatekeepers scan ten times more words and seven times more stories than the reader ever sees.

Two studies of what makes it through the gatekeepers offer even lower estimates for stories about discrimination and ethnoviolence. The first, conducted in Chicago in 1988–1989, scrutinized the daily and weekly Chicago papers, looking for reports of ethnoviolent crimes. The researchers compared these reports to those recorded by the Chicago Commission on Human Relations. The researchers, David L. Protess and James S. Ettema of Northwestern University, found that only 9 percent of ethnoviolent crimes reported to the Commission were mentioned in the press. Following their lead, the Prejudice Institute examined the *Sun* papers coverage of Maryland bias incidents over a three-and-a-half-year period, January 1990 through July 1993. The study compared their articles with reports made to the state Human Relations Commission by local police departments. The Institute found that for every eighty-two incidents only one was reported in either of the *Sun* papers. Of those reported, none could be called a "big picture" story. Although there is considerably more concern among editors and publishers about matters of race and ethnic relations today, these changes seem more related to meeting the new demographics of their market than to the politics of the situation. Some newspapers have initiated programs of diversity education for their staffs, but I doubt that the role of newspapers in communicating matters of intergroup relations has changed significantly.

The various journalism reviews and professional journals of communication are redundant with stories and examples of how gatekeepers do their gatekeeping—and anguish over it. (The Columbia Journalism Review, for example, ran back-to-back issues with articles about "the race beat," July–August and September–October 1999.) My purpose here is to adopt a unique perspective by viewing one dimension of newspaper policy and practice. Specifically, in part one of this report, we look at the assignment of reporters to stories of race and ethnic relations, how editors view such beats, and what they perceive to be the major problems in their community. To accomplish this, we interviewed the "assignment editors" from forty-eight of the fifty leading circulating daily newspapers in the United States during April–May 1999. The fifty were selected from the circulation data reported by Editor & Publisher, a trade journal. Twenty-seven million people read those papers. Of the fifty newspapers contacted, only the *New York Daily News* refused to be interviewed, and a *Milwaukee Journal-Sentinel* editor terminated the interview early (though after we had obtained our basic information). The *New York Post* editors would let only their public relations officer speak for them.

Although the people we interviewed had different titles, with one exception they all identified themselves as having the responsibility of assigning reporters to breaking stories. Their titles included managing editor, city editor, assistant city editor, metro editor, managing editor for news, senior editor, executive news editor, breaking news editor, and general assignment editor. When there were beat reporters who were generally free to choose their own stories, we interviewed the editors to whom they were responsible.

I started this research from the perspective that editors and reporters make the news. Editors decide who and what events are newsworthy. Veteran reporters and beat reporters are also implicated as newsmakers. For reporters, newsmaking is more complex since they have to tell a story that is acceptable to the editor (and possibly others in the news organization hierarchy) as well as those who were their sources and, often, the participants in the events being written about. In this first part I will not talk about the constraints on reporters but rather on how the editor as an institutional representative chooses the reporter and views group relations in their community.

Assigning Stories

> This newspaper takes this stuff seriously.
> —NEWS AIDE

I opened our interviews by asking editors the following: "Newspapers seem to use four different options when dealing with stories regarding race and ethnic relations. Which of the following is true of your paper?" The editors were then read four options and permitted to choose one or more. The options, which we present here in slightly abbreviated form, were: (a) the paper has a reporter assigned to a race and ethnic relations beat; (b) stories are assigned to a limited number of experienced reporters; (c) stories in this area are covered by reporters on other beats—for example, the religion reporter would cover the arson of a black church; (d) the story would likely be given to an available general assignment reporter. Of the forty-nine responses, twenty-seven editors (55 percent) identified their papers as having a special beat dedicated to reporting on issues of race and ethnic (R&E) relations. Five of the twenty-seven papers had more than one person assigned to that beat, ranging from two to five reporters. The titles and scope of the beats varied and seemed to reflect local concerns. The beat titles included race relations, minority affairs, urban affairs, immigrant relations, black issues, multicultural affairs, Hispanic affairs, and diverse communities.

Of the twenty-seven papers, two of the positions were vacant, one editor couldn't name the reporter, and another, oddly, refused to do so. At the most, then, about half the papers surveyed had a reporter assigned to a beat that specifically focused on intergroup relations.

Just because there is an R&E beat doesn't mean that editors give priority to those assigned to it. I asked editors which option they would choose first. Their answers are revealing:

- Call on other beat reporters first: 32 percent
- Call on the R&E beat reporter: 19 percent
- Depends on the story: 17 percent
- Call on an experienced reporter: 15 percent
- Call on a general-assignment reporter: 13 percent
- No answer: 4 percent

From our questions, it appears that even where there are R&E reporters, editors have less confidence in them than other beat reporters. For a breaking story of intergroup significance, editors are more likely to turn to writers knowledgeable about a "substantive" institution. For example, on many papers, the religion editor would be more likely called on than the R&E reporter to cover the arson of a black church.

"The minority affairs reporter is often called in to help on a story," said one assistant city editor, "because it is seldom that race is the only element of the story." As we shall show, only a small group of editors seemed to regard intergroup relations as a substantive field. One city editor's commentary reflected the opinion of many of his peers, "Race is a part of daily life, so all reporters should be able to cover it."

Running through our interviews, though not always directly articulated, is a polarity. At one end, a small majority of newspapers maintain an R&E beat—but only a small number of those beat reporters are the first choice of the assignment editor. At the other end are the editors who believe that all reporters should be knowledgeable of race, ethnic, and multicultural issues. One team leader said, "We no longer have a beat. We felt it was better to make sure every reporter could cover these types of stories." While many of the editors we spoke with would agree with this metro team leader, it was our impression that quite a few were trying to present a socially acceptable response. For them, an R&E beat smacked of special privilege and political correctness. They saw no substantial reason for such a beat.

Newspapers share many organizational features and these structural features often determine policy. Some have a big general-assignment staff, and for many of those all breaking stories go to a general-assignment reporter first. Other papers place more emphasis on team reporting as opposed to beat assignments. Finally, for some, the speed of events and the relentless deadlines mean, as one metro editor in charge of race and ethnic relations told us, "there are days we have to use anyone who's available."

Determining Who Is Qualified

"We match reporters' strengths to stories," one city editor told us. "Race relations knowledge is one of those strengths." Although he was not alone in regarding race and ethnic relations as having a distinctive body of knowledge, the editors interviewed were significantly divided in their attitudes towards an R&E beat. Some thought it was politically important to do so.

As a team leader for social issues remarked, "It is easy to say that race and ethnic stories will be covered, but they tend not to be. It is of critical importance that one person should be devoted to racial issues so the stories are covered properly and receive enough visibility."

I asked editors whether they thought special skills and knowledge were required to report about race and ethnic relations or whether they thought such stories were adequately covered by most general-assignment reporters. While seven of the editors declined to answer or answered equivocally, I was surprised by the diversity of replies from those who did comment. They were almost equally divided on the "special skills" versus "general assignment" choice, but they presented a more complex perspective on the issues.

Those advocating for general-assignment reporters tip their hats to knowledge and experience:

- City editor: "A seasoned reporter with experience is necessary, but special training or knowledge is not."
- City editor: "Having some knowledge in the area is usually helpful, but generally it can be handled by any general-assignment reporter."
- Deputy managing editor for news: "Don't think you have to be a member of an ethnic minority to cover race relations. You need to be an experienced general-assignment reporter."

One metro editor placed it clearly in a context of professionalism, "You have to have special skills to cover any beat, and if race becomes an issue you better be able to write about that too. I am opposed to having a few reporters who claim to be experts on ethnic relations. Every reporter should be able to cover this issue or any other issue that is involved in beat reporting."

Some editors see themselves as integral to the coverage by their selection of the right reporter for the story. As one managing editor stated, "It certainly helps to have a reporter that people can relate to—who looks like them or talks like them. But that doesn't mean a very good general-assignment reporter can't cover the story adequately. The answers aren't simple. You need to pick a good reporter first and foremost." A city editor put it succinctly, "I judge each reporter on their skills to cover and tell news in a compelling manner." For one assistant city editor, reporters' skills rest with their ability to transcend their position. "There are times when a reporter can handle a story like that through general knowledge and ability to empathize. A lot of it depends on class, being able to relate to different classes of people regardless of how much education or sociology the reporter has studied. So it depends on the characteristics of the reporter."

For two editors in different parts of the country, the question posed was irrelevant. One of them, a managing editor, commented, "The ethnic mix of this community is our driving force. Given our area, everyone has to be equipped to work across groups. One-third of staff are people of color; many are bilingual." Two other editors, by contrast, seem confused by the complexity of issues. "It depends upon the story," began a day city editor. "The Jasper incident [the incident in Jasper, Texas, involving the murder of a black man by dragging him behind a truck] could be covered by a general-assignment reporter, but affirmative action coverage would need someone with special knowledge in that area." An assistant managing editor also began, "It depends on the story," and offered the following contingency: "For example, some Asian stories require extensive background knowledge while others do not."

Does the paper need an R&E beat? Are special skills and knowledge required? About one of every four editors said "yes." One city editor observed that reporters need to have a special interest, while an assistant managing editor commented that "the individual reporter needs to drive the story, possess the background knowledge and an absence of denial that racism still exists." A team leader noted that an R&E beat was too broad an assignment. The best approach, she said, was to have "the beat reporter on hand to give demographics and the sociological perspective."

The multiplicity of perspectives and the lack of consensus reflect two levels of concern. One level is that of professionalism and the differing perspectives concerning specialization and general practice. The other is that of the editors' knowledge base, or sociological sophistication. For some the vicissitudes of intergroup relations, cultural differences, and group conflicts are simply part of the urban landscape, which any good reporter can navigate. For others, the landscape calls for a knowledgeable guide who has the information to comprehend and transcend the cultures and conflicts.

List of Qualifications

For the twenty-seven newspapers with R&E beats, I asked the editors if the R&E reporters had any "specialized qualifications for this beat." Two-thirds of the editors said that they did. However, when I probed for what these were, their responses put a different twist on our question—unless you regard being black as a specialized qualification. Six of the editors said they did not know or declined to answer. Those who did cited an average of about two reasons:

- Being black or Hispanic or knowing Spanish: 32 percent
- Being an experienced reporter: 24 percent
- Having multicultural, multiethnic, urban experience: 16 percent
- Specific training (such as seminars or conferences): 14 percent
- Personal interest: 8 percent
- All other responses: 6 percent

The picture that begins to surface among even these editors, where an R&E beat is established, is the view of this domain as requiring little mastery beyond one's ethnicity or intergroup experiences. There is no sense that this is a field in which expertise counts—or exists. The general feeling is that a seasoned reporter can cover any story, and that little of any special value is to be found in the sociology of intergroup relations.

What Editors Know

> I think [people of color] have pretty much
> attained social and political equality.
> MANAGING EDITOR

Consider the question: "What do you think are the most important problems of race and ethnic relations facing your community?" Take a breath, give yourself one minute, and name as many important problems as you can. If you named more than two, you exceeded the median number of problems identified by our sample of editors. If you named more than three, you identified more than ninety percent of the editors. I was not expecting a sociological discourse, but I was taken aback by the lack of sophistication of our respondents.

To begin with, many of the editors were nonplussed. "The question is too general for me to answer" (assistant city editor); "Can't say right now" (city editor); "I'd have to think about it" (assistant metro editor). An assistant managing editor evaded the question by declaring, "I would rather not answer free-form questions," while a deputy managing editor sidestepped with, "Race and ethnic relations is a major issue in this country."

The banality of many of the answers bordered on parody. "Lack of understanding" (day city editor); "People are suspicious of each other" (city editor); "Communication—not enough back and forth" (city editor). A managing editor offered this maxim, "[This] is a very diverse place, so tolerance, understanding, and diversity are all crucial." Or, as a general assignment editor put it, "In any community there is always a failure to empathize or understand people who are different."

A few editors seemed genuinely out of touch. According to a deputy bureau chief, "The only really big problem in this city is perceived racial brutality by police. There are no racial problems in schools or housing." One state editor saw the problem being generated by those who were victims. "The Hispanic population tends not to be as successful at equipping itself with fundamental skills achieved through schooling."

About one out of five editors were able to articulately present the problems of their community in a straightforward manner. To us, what is significant is not whether their analysis is "correct" but that they have thought about the problems their reporters write about:

- Managing news editor: "The most important is the housing costs in [this city]. They are going through the roof and this will mostly affect minorities. Second is job training. Third is education. Fourth is political clout which delivers everything else."
- Breaking news editor: "Residential segregation. Racial prejudice in hiring. There is an underlying racial prejudice that skews the distribution of resources and results in a majority of minorities living in poverty."

Two metro editors specifically cited the role of the newspaper as part of the problems they see:

Race impacts everything in this community. There is a problem integrating all the races that have come in. It is no longer just a black and white issue. There has been a huge expansion of a black middle class, but you do not see this reflected in the newspapers. Black people are portrayed as poor . . .

There is not enough explanation in the media as to how groups are similar. So, we end up fearing the unknown. We need to show similarities; the differences should be interesting, not divides. We need to show we are a homogeneous society, even though we come from different parts of the world.

Sydney Schanberg, an investigations editor, wrote that to bring newspapers to a serious examination of ethics and quality, they will need to create a "press beat."[1] Perhaps so, but we have seen that those assigned to an R&E beat are not always called upon and that their training is informal and inadequate. Perhaps, most significantly, is that the editors they report to are themselves not a knowledgeable crew.

Concluding Remarks

> We need to make sure that people see
> themselves portrayed honestly in the paper.
> CITY EDITOR

Over and again, editors remarked that race and ethnicity were so important, so integral to the community, that every reporter should be sensitive to the issues. Surely this is a true statement, but it is also self-deluding. Should every reporter be an environmentalist? A business reporter? A crime reporter? A city hall reporter? Any educated and solid reporter would be "sensitive" to those domains so integral to the community, but no one would expect expertise in all of them.

What are the consequences of not having an R&E beat reporter? Or, to put it positively, what can a solid beat reporter do? We can expect that beat reporters can travel with ease within the communities they cover. We can expect that not only do they know those communities and the key influentials, but that they also have a network of informants and sources with whom they can deal. It takes time to learn about a subcultural community, to get to be known and trusted. With the knowledge and access that a beat reporter can develop, editors could expect and readers could enjoy a level of expert enterprise reporting that the typical general-assignment reporter would be locked out of.

Ideally, the R&E beat reporter would have another level of knowledge to build on: a knowledge of the dynamics of prejudice and intergroup relations.

For example, the beat reporter trained in this area would easily recognize this article as a discourse on discrimination. The trained beat reporter would know that frustration does not really lead to aggression, that personality is not the cause of prejudice, that ethnoviolence may be more traumatic than other forms of violence, that discrimination is a necessary condition of group conflict, that race is a social construct, that affirmative action quotas have to be court-ordered and that this has been a rare occurrence, that Ebonics is a natural language with rules sometimes more complex than standard English, and that prejudiced attitudes are easy to change. And much more.

What I have just cited is a mishmash of findings, but only when statements such as these are common knowledge would a race and ethnicity beat be redundant.

STUDY TWO: THE REPORTERS

The Prejudice Institute's study looked at the characteristics of reporters who write about race and ethnic group relations—who they are, what training they have, how they view the problems of civil rights and ethnoviolence, and what effect this has had on them personally.

We began with telephone calls to the hundred leading circulating daily newspapers, asking to talk with reporters who had a race beat. Where the paper had no such beat, we asked to talk with an experienced general-assignment reporter who regularly wrote about matters of race and ethnic relations. We discovered two things immediately: that newspapers often became very defensive when asked that question and—as our earlier study indicated—close to half the papers had no such beat. (The names of such beats are highly varied and often euphemistically labeled, for example, the "city beat.") We obtained names from various levels of editors and, occasionally, from other reporters. Although only a few people refused to be interviewed, many of our conversations had a level of edginess and a great reluctance to answer some "opinion" questions. In all, we completed sixty-six interviews, thirty-six with beat reporters and thirty with general-assignment reporters.

In the "perfect newsroom," the differences between a beat reporter and a general-assignment reporter should be minimal. Manifestly, the exception should be that the beat reporter would be more knowledgeable about the subject of her or his beat. As this study shows, there are many points of similarity. However, beat reporters experience and define their jobs in a somewhat different manner, experience more conflict with their editors, and have different attitudes regarding their paper's performance and some civil rights issues.

The top fifty newspapers were slightly more likely than the smaller papers to have reporters assigned to a race beat. The difference can be easily attributed to staff size. Both the beat and nonbeat groups are equally experienced, averaging between twelve to thirteen years on the job. However, the beat reporters said they spend 80 percent of their time working on their beat while general-assignment reporters said that they are called on only one-third of the time to cover race/ethnic issues.

The two groups had no difference in gender composition. Approximately 52 percent were women. With regard to race/ethnicity, there was a significant difference.[2] Only 6 percent of the beat reporters are white. Table 5.1 presents their distribution, highlighting the fact that even general-assignment reporters who are white are less likely to be called on for a story in this area.

Table 5.1 Beat and General Assignment Reporters by Race/Ethnicity

Race/ethnicity	Beat Reporters		General Assignment Reporters	
	n	%	n	%
Black	17	47.2	12	42.9
Latino	11	30.6	4	14.3
Other minority	6	16.7	1	3.6
White	2	5.6	11	39.3
Totals	36.0	100.1	28.0	100.1

Further, given the relatively small proportion of minorities generally in the newsroom, Table 5.1 indicates a considerable level of segregation by assignment. Moreover, the Newspaper Publishers Association reports that whites make up 80 percent of the newsroom.

Beat Assignment

Race beat reporting is probably not high in newsroom prestige. As we observed in the first study, most editors did not regard this as a preeminent area of specialization. Nevertheless, reporters took on this beat voluntarily. Two-thirds of them applied or were asked to create the position. In general, the race beat went to those who pursued it, and most were women and minorities. Reporters themselves were often instrumental in establishing the beat. One illustration is the case of an esteemed black reporter on a major paper. The editors on hearing that she had been made a job offer by another leading paper asked what it would take for her to stay. She replied that she would stay if they allowed her to set up a race beat. They agreed but said she could do so only on a six-month trial. They did not believe there was enough news to sustain a beat reporter. She left after a year and the beat was then abandoned.

We asked both the beat and general-assignment reporters if they had any special training that prepared them for writing about race and ethnic relations. A small majority of reporters said that they had taken special training, with twice as many beat reporters as general-assignment reporters indicating such training. About one-third of the training experiences cited were university courses, including majors and minors in race relations curricula. Two-thirds of the experiences were seminars taken on the job. Many reporters who had no formal training mentioned personal experiences and "just living it" as their learning base.

We approached the issue of training another way as well. We asked our sample, "If you were hiring a reporter for your paper to cover immigration and race relations, what questions would you ask, what qualifications would you look for?" Although four reporters said that they would look for nothing special, the sixty-two remaining reporters were voluble on the matter, producing over two hundred discrete comments. The researchers were able to classify their comments into eight relatively exclusive categories. "Reportorial skills and experience" was cited by almost three out of four respondents. Almost as many, 69 percent, specified minority and diverse cultural experience as a major qualification for the assignment. None of the remaining categories included more than one-third of the reporters.

When we compared the responses of beat reporters and general-assignment reporters, however, an interesting though not surprising pattern emerged. While almost all reporters mentioned matters of professional skill and competency, the beat reporters were significantly more likely to emphasize matters relating to prejudice and intergroup experiences. In addition, they were more likely to raise the issues of a candidates' views on prejudice and race, their being free of prejudice, how they would go about working in minority communities, their curiosity, openness, and desire to learn about cultural differences, and whether they were bilingual.

On the Job

> They wanted me to write white.
> BLACK WOMAN BEAT REPORTER

Most reporters were expected to develop their own stories. The beat reporters were considerably less likely to be assigned stories than were their general-assignment counterparts. We asked our respondents, "What are the obstacles you face from editors or managers of the newspaper in covering the stories?" There were significant differences in their answers. General-assignment reporters were twice as likely to reply that there were "no obstacles," 43 percent of them as compared to 22 percent of beat reporters. In contrast, beat reporters were almost twice as likely to identify their editors as a major obstacle, 58 percent as compared to 30 percent. To the beat reporters, the editors often could not see the importance of the stories they were covering. Even when they could, they were "afraid of offending white readers." One quarter attributed the obstacles they faced to the "lack of minorities in high positions."

We also explored the issue of editorial control. Specifically, we asked if an editor had seriously changed or refused to run a story. Although there were significant differences between the two groups, there were also more refusals and evasive answers to this question than any other in the interview schedule. Slightly more than half of the general-assignment reporters maintained that their stories had never been seriously changed. In contrast, one-third of the beat reporters said that they had stories that were seriously changed, moved to the back pages, or killed. One reporter commented that these changes were "too many to count." Overall, the reporters' responses highlight the underlying intergroup tensions. Note how the theme of differential perception plays through these comments:

- Like most papers, [this one] is run by white males who feel there is no appeal for these issues to white suburban readers.
- Whites do not understand the importance of these stories.
- I had a perspective from my background. They wanted me to write white.

- There were editors who wanted [me] to be more sensitive to their white readership and who didn't want to offend them by printing certain stories.
- My editor refused to run a story, claiming it is working on an old topic.
- White editors tend to think that race is discussed too much in the news.

Another recurring theme is the editors' avoidance of controversy. Editors are seen as not wanting to offend, as wanting to do the right thing, and as avoiding giving expression to radical views. "News," one journalist said, "is what the editors see on their way to work."

In the Community

We asked the open-ended question, "What do you think are the most important problems of race and ethnic relations facing your community?' The question yielded close to three hundred responses—a median of nearly five responses per person. It was apparent that these issues were at the forefront of this select group of journalists. The responses of the reporters stood in sharp contrast to the editors' survey. The median response rate to this question by editors was two, and many of their responses were nonspecific.

General-assignment and beat reporters both identified the same set of issues, with economic inequality being cited by almost fifty percent. The five most frequently mentioned issues were

- economic inequality;
- group hostility, prejudice;
- schools, educational inequality;
- residential segregation;
- whites not adapting to demographic changes.

Although these comments did provide labels for the major issues, they were, nevertheless, descriptive. Few reporters went beyond this labeling. Not only was there consensus between the general-assignment and beat reporters, but this was equally true when the data was examined by race/ethnicity and gender.

We included two attitudinal questions, asking, first, whether the reporters thought the push for minority rights was "too fast, not fast enough, [or] about right." There was a strong tendency, though not statistically significant, for beat reporters to regard civil rights activism as not moving fast enough (56 percent of beat reporters versus 42 percent of general-assignment reporters). The second question we posed dealt with the imposition of enhanced penalties for hate crimes. Here, too, there was no significant difference. A substantial majority of both groups favored enhanced penalties.

So, in the identification of community problems, their view of the speed of the push for civil rights, and the use of enhanced penalties, beat and general-assignment reporters were not easily distinguished. What about their view of the coverage given these issues by their newspaper? We queried, "These days do you think your newspaper writes too much about race, too little about race, or about the right amount about race?" One reporter said "too much," while 69 percent of the beat reporters and 53 percent of the general-assignment reporters said "too little." Again, we observed a substantial but not statistically significant difference.

Personal Changes

We closed by asking our sample whether their experience in this area had resulted in their changing their views of race/ethnic relations. The differences between the two groups were complex and interesting. The general-assignment reporters were twice as likely to claim that their writing in this area had not affected their views. Beyond that, one-third of both groups felt that covering these stories had enhanced their knowledge of race/ethnic relations. Many reporters felt "more pessimistic" and "cynical." Others felt more accepting, less likely to stereotype, and more aware of the difficulties of talking about race relations; some were more appreciative of issues of social class. In all, beat reporters seemed more open; to have experienced more changes and a greater mix of changes; and—in the words of several reporters—to have a less idealistic approach to these social issues.

Basic Findings

These two modest studies exposed manifest and covert tensions that pervade the newsroom over the reporting of race and ethnic issues. These are the major findings:

1. Approximately two out of five newsrooms have no R&E beat.
2. Despite the fact that beat reporters are as experienced as their general-assignment counterparts *and* have greater training in their specialty, the likelihood is low that they would be called on first by an editor to cover a breaking story concerning intergroup relations.
3. Most editors and reporters emphasize their professionalism in selecting reporters and matching them to beats or to stories. However, once this mantra is set aside, beat reporters are more likely to assert the importance of intergroup experience and training. They are also more likely than others to emphasize the significance of being free of prejudice.
4. Among editors, there is no sense of the sociology of group relations or, presumably, a need for that knowledge. Being black or being able to speak Spanish seems more critical.
5. When asked about the problems of race and ethnic relations in their communities, the editors set themselves apart from the reporters. The median number of problems they were aware of was two, and only 10 percent recognized more than three problems. Moreover, many of the so-called problems cited by editors were often banalities such as "lack of understanding." Reporters, in sharp contrast, identified twice as many problems. While their responses covered the range of institutional injustices, they lacked an analytic specificity.
6. Beat reporters tend to be more critical of the progress of civil rights in society and the coverage given such issues by their newspaper.
7. On the matter of editorial control, beat and general-assignment reporters had considerably different impressions. The R&E writers were significantly more likely to report that they had stories that were seriously changed, buried, or killed. Further, the reporters perceived these changes to be a consequence of white editors who did not understand the issues or were attempting to avoid alienating white readers.

Concluding Remarks

The reporters we interviewed were experienced journalists, pretty much acting on the same basic set of journalistic values, highly valuing reportorial skills and experience. This professionalism frequently overrode their race, ethnicity, and gender. Nevertheless, the R&E reporters were considerably more sensitive to matters of prejudice and intergroup experience.

They often regarded their editors as insensitive to the issues of race and ethnic relations and overly concerned with not giving offense to white readers. They were more likely to have had an editor who blocked or seriously changed what they had written.

When we looked at the reporters' diagnosis of the problems facing their communities, we were again reminded of their similarity in perspective, although R&E reporters were more likely to feel the need for greater coverage of race and ethnic issues. In fact, beat reporters sought opportunities to write about their subject and had taken college courses and other training to enhance their knowledge. In their statements about community problems, they reiterated what could have been the chapter headings of a race relations textbook. In their replies, there was almost a script-like quality. In part, it may be that the researchers were looking for the reporters' analysis, while the reporters were "stuck" at a lower level of description. For the editors, even the descriptors seemed elusive.

The editors, with a few exceptions, were reluctant partners in the interviews. In general they regarded their function as gatekeepers as a nonissue. They felt no need for special competencies that went beyond journalistic experience. It is not surprising, then, that beat reporters experienced a decided tension between themselves and their editors.

This data, though modest, suggests a need for two interventions. The first is that of bringing editors and beat reporters together to share perspectives. The second is a much needed basic set of seminars focusing on the *analysis* (as distinguished from description) of the issues of race and ethnic relations. Going beyond this is the design of research that looks specifically at the differences in style and content as reflected in stories written by beat and general-assignment reporters. Finally, conspicuously absent from this research venue is the impact of content on readership.

NOTES

1. Sydney Schanberg, "The News No One Dares to Cover," *Washington Post,* August 29, 1999.

2. We use the term *significant* here and throughout this report to signify statistical significance as well as substantive significance. A difference between categories, in this case beat and nonbeat, is statistically significant if its likelihood of occurrence by chance is less than five times in one hundred. The actual statistical tests, usually chi square, are available from the authors.

6

THE PRODUCTION OF PATHOLOGY
The Social Function of Local TV News

WRITTEN WITH JASON WELLER

The National Advisory Commission on Civil Disorders has written that

> Along with the country as a whole, the press has too long basked in a white world, looking out of it, if at all, with the white men's eyes and a white perspective. That is no longer good enough. The painful process of readjustment that is required of the American news media must begin now. They must make a reality of integration in both their product and personnel. They must insist on the highest standards of accuracy—not only reporting single events with care and skepticism, but placing each event into a meaningful perspective.[1]

This report and proposal is part of the news media research program of the Prejudice Institute. In this chapter we focus on the treatment of race/ethnicity, gender, and violence in local television news. We have three objectives: a review of the disparate research literature, a proposal and design for replicating the major findings, and the development of a new interpretive framework that shifts focus to institutional discrimination and its pathological consequences for the social capital of the local community.

Why study television news? First, it is the commonplace observation that in a democracy, news is critical to an informed citizen. Yet, even as we nod to the obvious, we need to acknowledge that the mass media of communications are becoming increasingly concentrated. Ben Bagdikian, in his classic book *The Media Monopoly,* now in its ninth edition, shows that less than half a dozen corporate leviathans control most American media.[2] It is worth noting that in the first edition, in 1983, the corresponding figure was fifty corporations. James Surowiecki, writing in the *New Yorker*, graphically describes the concentration. "Big media players control both programming and distribution. Five companies own all the broadcast networks, four of the major movie studios, and ninety percent of the top fifty cable channels. These companies also produce three-quarters of all prime-time programming."[3]

This concentration of ownership and the character of the content of news programs have had particular consequences for American society. Robert W. McChesney and John Nichols note: "Still top-heavy with white middle-class men, TV news departments and major newspapers remain in thrall to official sources. Their obsessive focus on crime coverage and celebrity trials leaves no room for covering the real issues that affect neighborhoods and whole classes of people. Coverage of communities of color, women, gays, and lesbians, rural folks and just about everyone else who doesn't live in a handful of ZIP codes in New York and Los Angeles is badly warped, and it creates badly warped attitudes in society."[4]

Television is an integral part of American culture and society. It plays a pivotal role in the dissemination of news. A 2004 Gallup Poll reported that local television news is the most used of all the daily news sources. Local television news ranks at the top of the list of daily news sources, with 51 percent of Americans saying they use this source every day (and another 19 percent saying they use it several times a week). Local newspapers received a 44 percent daily use ranking and cable news programs were cited by 39 percent. An interesting sidebar to the survey was the finding that daily local TV news viewing increases directly with age: 33 percent of eighteen- to twenty-nine-year-olds; 50 percent of thirty- to forty-nine-year-olds; 51 percent of fifty- to sixty-four-year-olds; and 70 percent of those sixty-five and older.

The image of the world that is portrayed by the news media and presumably consumed by viewers has come under heavy criticism for reflecting the values and opinions of a homogenized "white world."[5] Since the National Advisory Commission on Civil Disorders findings nearly thirty-six years ago, the portrayal of traditional minorities on television shows has become a focus of academic research as well as a cause for various minority defense agencies. The daily news programs are no exception to this trend. As Campbell (1995) points out, blacks in the news are typically placed into one of three roles: criminals, victims, and celebrities.[6] To many critics these stylized portrayals simply fit within the framework of the media as a means to perpetuate the status quo of the dominant white society.[7]

Television news and entertainment frames the world for its viewers, and many viewers come to believe what they see on the screen. For example, despite the fact that violent crime rates have been in steady decline, the prolonged viewing of local news with its unremitting coverage of crime and mayhem leads to an increase in concern over crime. Crime is the most common topic in the news by a margin of two to one.[8] Moreover, the awareness of crime contributes to an overall belief that the world is a dangerous place,[9] thus eroding the social capital of viewers. Gerbner's studies of prime-time programs indicate, furthermore, that prolonged television viewing leads to the belief that violence is an appropriate response to conflict.

Many critics argue that television has simply become another device to perpetuate stereotypes and validate intergroup relations.[10] Current studies of TV news have established a significant trend in reporting: the connection of race and crime. Chiricos and Escholz summarized the major finding of their case study of Orlando, Florida, television: "When all persons appearing on TV news programs are considered, including reporters and anchors, 1 in 20 Whites who appear on screen is a crime suspect. More than 1 in 8 Blacks and more than 1 in 4 Hispanics who appear on the screen during Orlando news programs are suspects of crimes. This is one clear indicator of the criminal typification of race and ethnicity."[11]

Even black community leaders and politicians cannot escape stereotype assignment. Often when they appear on the news they are shown in an oppositional stance. Whether calling attention to discriminatory acts or demanding action from government officials, they are often framed as malcontents.[12]

Gilliam and Iyengar provide another perspective. They assert that images of blacks and Hispanics as violent criminals are unrepresentative: "The media's near exclusive focus on violent crime distorts the real world in the following way: when viewers encounter a suspect in the news he is invariably a violent perpetrator, when in reality the greatest number of felony arrests are for *property* crimes." Typically when nonviolent crimes are covered the criminals are White, although in reality "minorities actually account for the largest share of nonviolent (property) felonies."[13]

Entman, in his research program, has focused on the way that young black males are portrayed as violent criminals. The results of his findings have been twofold. First is the "racialization of crime": If certain crimes are mentioned, an immediate assumption is that the perpetrators were black men. Second is the differential portrayal of black versus white criminals. Black suspects are more likely to be seen wearing prison garb, in handcuffs, and in the physical grasp of guards, whereas whites are more likely to be seen wearing business attire, unrestrained, and in the company of their attorneys.[14]

THE LATINO PRESENCE

Most of the research dealing with Latinos has concentrated on the entertainment media. However, one important survey conducted by the National Association of Hispanic Journalists examined the portrayal of Latinos in network television news. Specifically, the survey examined the network evening newscasts—ABC, NBC, CBS, and CNN—for the entire year of 2002. Latino-related stories made up less than 1 percent of all the stories appearing in the network newscasts. Of that number, two-thirds of the stories focused on crime, terrorism, and illegal immigration. As the report notes, "Latinos continued to be portrayed as a dysfunctional underclass that exists on the fringes of mainstream U.S. society."[15] The marginalization of Latinos was so comprehensive that in three out of four Latino-related stories, only Anglos were interviewed.

In their analysis of local newscasts in Orlando, Florida—a city with a substantial Latino population—Chiricos and Escholz found that Latinos were more likely to appear as violent crime suspects than for crimes in general and were more likely than whites and blacks to appear as criminal suspects. Finally, the researchers found that Latinos were the least likely to appear as positive role models.[16]

THE INVISIBLE WOMAN

Almost all research has focused on race/ethnicity, crime, and violence, seriously ignoring the appearance of women in local news. For example,

Weibel, despite her comprehensive historical survey of the images of women in popular culture, has nothing to say about women in the news except to note that the first female news anchor (Barbara Walters) did not appear until 1976.[17]

The appearance of women in TV news is paradoxical. In the United States, 39 percent of all television news jobs are held by women, and more than one-fourth of all news directors are women.[18] Virtually all the data about women in the news derives from studies of the network evening news conducted from 1 January to 31 December 2001. (The programs were *ABC World News Tonight, NBC Nightly News,* and *CBS Evening News.*) The researchers, Media Tenor, Ltd, analyzed 18,765 individual news reports. Their primary focus was on who was selected as a source for on-camera interviews. Their overall finding was not surprising. "Network news demonstrated a clear tendency to showcase the opinions of the most powerful political and economic actors, while giving limited access to those voices that would be most likely to challenge them."[19]

The three networks had only minor differences. More than half the women (52 percent) who appeared in the news were displayed as average citizens. This was not true of male sources, who appeared as average citizens only 14 percent of the time. Women, moreover, comprised only 19 percent of sources. Men were clearly the authoritative voice; women were nonexperts. Of special note is the coverage of gender-related stories such as equal opportunity, abortion rights, and discrimination. "Women were presented as nonexpert citizens 77 percent of the time in gender-related stories. Men, by contrast, spoke as experts in their fields 100 percent of the time in such stories."[20]

Overall, women find themselves in a more precarious position than people of color when it comes to their representation in television news. As Rakow and Kranich argue, women's roles are created and circumscribed by men, therefore they are empty and meaningless.[21] Similar to Entman's findings,[22] Rakow and Kranich in their analysis of one month of transcripts from the evening news on ABC, NBC, and CBS also found that women's roles in television is stereotypic: Women are portrayed neither as newsmakers nor as sources. Moreover, women do not appear as experts about women's issues: "They cannot escape their femininity, yet the possibility of making a contribution that is specifically on behalf of women is ruled out. They may not speak as women or for women."[23] Rakow and

Kranich also cite the media as contributing to the notion that feminism is a white women's movement: "On the rare occasions that news media personnel choose to incorporate a feminist perspective on a news story, they go to familiar, predominantly white, liberal, visible organizations." Perhaps most telling of all is Rakow and Kranich's assertion that the portrayal of women and people of color as miscreants and troublemakers is used to the advantage of the status quo: "Oppressive actions against women and men of other races are justified and their threat to the social order quelled when they are presented as inherently dangerous and disruptive."[24]

THE TWELVE-MINUTE HALF HOUR

Of the thirty minutes that are allotted for the presentation of the news, approximately twelve to fifteen minutes are actually spent on presenting news stories. Despite all the work that goes into creating a newscast, Graber states that the news content in the thirty-minute broadcast is comparable to that found in a single page of a newspaper.[25] The Project for Excellence in Journalism found that 70 percent of local television news stories are one minute or shorter.[26] Klite, Bardwell, and Salzman found that the average news story lasts forty-seven seconds. The most time is committed to commercials, program promotion, weather, sports, and cheery banter between the anchors.[27]

Because of its traditional reliance on on-the-scene footage, television news requires staff who can arrive at the scene and get the footage and interviews in time for broadcast. Not any footage, of course. The focus is on spectacles, especially crime, but also fires, disasters, and severe weather. These account for 61 percent of the leads in the two thousand four hundred broadcasts studied by the Project for Excellence in Journalism. The result is a reliance on repeated film clips—local, network, and independent—and reporters "with a live update from the newsroom."

One of the primary effects of this kind of presentation of the news is the lack of a historical context for the stories.[28] To understand how this process plays out daily in the news, consider a story of a fire in a low-income housing project. In all likelihood, the fire itself would be the subject of the story and there would not be any discussion of how and why housing projects came into existence. Assigning an investigative team to look into this is risky, time-consuming, and expensive. Keeping stories to less than a minute is much cheaper than committing staff to lengthy research assignments.[29]

Many writers note that the news media points the viewer to what is important by positioning a story, by allotting a longer air time to a story, and by repeating a story, or a teaser about a story, several times throughout the newscast. As paradoxical as it may seem, newscasts devote a large amount of time to self-promotion. The Rocky Mt. Group, in their study of local newscasts, found that teasers get "more airtime than that devoted to any single news topic except crime."[30]

An interesting facet of these broadcasts is that little is left to chance, including the dialogue between an anchor and a reporter, which is often scripted and rehearsed before going live.[31] An "uninformed" viewer may see this dialogue and conclude that the anchor is engaging critically in the story and questioning the information that the reporter is providing. This process thus assists with providing legitimacy to the story as well as to the newscast, an idea that is supported by a national survey in which 54 percent of the respondents said they have a great deal or a fair amount of "trust and confidence" that the media is "reporting the news fully, accurately, and fairly."[32] Black viewers, more than whites, are critical of the news and especially racial issues within the news.

Give the People What They Want?

Many program directors simply claim that they are giving viewers what they want. In contrast to this claim, Gerbner found that when people were given a choice between violent and nonviolent content, they typically chose the nonviolent.[33] Station managers also cite budgetary constraints as a major factor that perpetuates stories being less than a minute long.

Lack of ethnic and cultural diversity in TV news management may also be an important factor in deciding what gets aired. Presently, white males predominate as officials and managers of television stations.[34] A study conducted by Lind found that when a racially diverse group of individuals was asked to construct a news program from a list of stories, blacks and whites identified very different stories to cover.[35] In response to this issue, Wilson and Gutierrez suggest that greater racial/ethnic diversity in higher-level positions will allow more people a significant voice on who and what is portrayed in the media.[36]

We Are Living in a Material World

The primary intended and recognized function (what sociologists call the *manifest function*) of local news is to sell advertising time for consumer goods and services. A station's revenues depend on its ability to draw an audience at the least cost to itself. The coverage of crime and spectacles bolstered by the weather report and sports has become the conventional mode for organizing the news program and enticing viewers. The standard TV industry claim is that they are presenting what the viewing audience wants. (Although the claim is not well documented, local news programming is highly profitable.) In contrast, in seven surveys conducted from 1975 to 1997, most respondents indicate their dissatisfaction with violent programming.[37]

Postman and Powers engaged in a critical examination of the way that commercialization has affected news programs. They concluded that the evening news is presented in such a way that it keeps viewers' attention long enough to get them to the next commercial break.[38] Similarly, in a thirty-minute clip of a CNN broadcast, Harris found that there were 289 ads and logos on the screen as endorsements, product placements, and overt advertisements.[39] Klite, Bardwell, and Salzman report that in some markets, a thirty-minute news program has as much as twelve minutes of commercial time.[40] The Project for Excellence in Journalism noted an average of fourteen stories, with some stations airing as few as seven stories per night and one station typically airing twenty-seven stories. In a few cases more time was allocated to commercials than to the news itself.[41]

Aside from the obvious profits generated by local news programs, commercials serve two significant sociological functions. First, the commercial releases the viewer from grim and violent news, transporting the viewer back to life as usual. Second, the frequency of commercials, and their often attention-getting power, fragments the news. Not only does the newscast fail to focus on the issues, as opposed to the events, but it provides no space for the viewer to do so. One consequence of the news as presented is that it confuses people.

We need to remind ourselves that the effects of watching TV news are not uniform across an audience. Chiricos and associates argue that the viewers' life experiences affect the way that they interpret the news: "The issue is not whether media accounts of crime increase fear, but which audiences, with which experiences and interests, construct which meanings from the messages received."[42] Viewers will perceive the news in ways that makes sense to them. One example noted by Chiricos was the fear response of white women when they viewed "women like themselves" as victims on the news.

A CRITICAL SOCIOLOGICAL PERSPECTIVE

Viewed from the standpoint of a critical sociologist, local television news functions to present short stories that offer the viewer an interpretation of the world from the security of home. It validates the viewer's perception of the world primarily by reinforcing the legitimacy of the sociopolitical system. That is, it tells people that everything is really okay and that life goes on as usual. More than that, with its overbearing focus on crime, it reminds people that this is a good society in which deviants will be punished.[43]

The newscast conceptualized in its entirety is a performance piece—entertainment held together by a familiar structure and the banter of the news anchors, the weatherperson, and the sportscaster. Of special interest to us here is that TV news presents the relations of dominant and subordinate groups in society without question. The main process by which it does so is the treatment of news as an event typically without a history or a social causation. The socioeconomic discrepancies among minority and dominant groups are drawn in three ways. First, by generally ignoring minorities; second, by depicting them in their limited appearances predominantly as criminals, victims, malcontents, or filler; and third, by the selection of white males as authority figures. What people view, then, is a set of visual narratives that reaffirm the workings of society.

Journalists decide what they think is newsworthy and, in doing so, make the news. Correspondingly, the television news program is a construction of events which by their presentation on the air become newsworthy. This idea is also supported by Lipschultz: "Local television news constructions essentially distribute knowledge to a local community in ways that influence decision making, create a 'dominant' social product, and lead to a social construction of reality that 'steers public policy.'"[44] One of the effects of this "steering of public policy" is the marginalization of minority news because it does not fit within the interests of mainstream white males.[45] Some critics conceptualize the mainstreaming of television as a structural issue. Jeffrey Scheuer, for example, asserts that in its very structure, television is a conservative medium. Television's major systematic effect is "simplification," he writes. The absence of the coverage of issues is a consequence of TV's inescapable rejection of ambiguity and complexity and its tendency toward emotional imagery. Thus, the structure itself leads to a bias in favor of the status quo.[46]

The past study of television news has, like the news itself, a narrow focus. Its primary focus has been on the consequences of the news in its portrayal of race/ethnicity and violence and in its rendering of women as irrelevant. Its secondary focus has been on the structure of the newscast itself. Here researchers have examined the amount of time allocated to various news sources. For example, how long was the news hole (the time available to report the story)? Did it cover the statehouse, the city council, the environment? What about sports and the weather? Were there warm and fuzzy stories? How much time did the anchors spend in small talk? Where it focused on race/ethnicity in particular, it had not gone much beyond observations of manifest content.

With a few exceptions, television news research has been done on a case study basis. That is, researchers have been limited usually to a single city and sometimes to a single TV station. This does not necessarily affect the quality of the study, but it does affect its generalizability. Thus, when we observe inconsistencies between the studies of Chicago and Orlando (Entman versus Chiricos),[47] we cannot determine whether they are methodologically generated or solid observations of differences in news coverage. Furthermore, almost all research has focused on differences between blacks and whites, ignoring class, gender, and other ethnicities. From an operational standpoint, these matters can be easily corrected by better sampling and a broader protocol for analyzing the manifest content of the newscasts.

The fact is, however, that the focus on manifest content is misleading, though patently important. We contend that the significance of the local newscast is much broader than these studies would lead you to believe. The media critic Mark Crispin Miller comes closest to articulating the toxic effect of the news. His examination of the crime coverage of the five major Baltimore stations led him to conclude:

Local television news' excessive emphasis on crime is steadily killing the very city it covers. While crime is a reality on the urban scene, the daily televised prominence of gore and violence in the broadcast news—the "if it bleeds, it leads formula"—is inadvertently bleeding the life and wealth out of Baltimore.[48]

The local TV newscast has an impact, as Miller suggests, well beyond its manifest content. As we have seen, it reaffirms the status structure in society by its racialization of crime and violence, by its depiction of minority leaders as malcontents, by the invisibility and low status of women and the concomitant selection of white males as authority figures, and by its marginalization of dissent. From the perspective of the community, local TV news fails to provide serious reporting on issues as opposed to events, and what it does cover is done in the context of fast-paced sound bites and short visuals sandwiched between commercials, program promotions, and teasers concerning upcoming news coverage.

The unintended and unrecognized consequences of a social institution—its *latent functions*—are typically removed from its stated mission. In this case, we view the latent function of the local news program as depleting the social capital of the community. In the structure of news programming and its underlying policies, TV news reaffirms social discrimination independent of the intent of the institution or the manner in which it does so. Further, in our model, discrimination is a necessary condition for ethnoviolence.

THE FINDINGS SO FAR

From past research, we can draw the following generalizations; some are well-confirmed and others more tentative:

- The protagonists of news stories (newsmakers) and central characters in news stories are predominantly white Anglo males. The minor characters are predominantly people of color and women.
- News stories are predominantly nonlocal.
- The predominant categories of stories (standard fare) are events rather than issues and are generally not stories of public affairs or general community relevance. In addition, people of color and women are overrepresented in standard fare stories. (Overrepresented here refers to a comparison with white males.)
- Black and Latino males are overrepresented in their appearance as criminal suspects and as suspects in violent crimes. People of color

and women are overrepresented as victims of crimes, disasters, and accidents.

- Women and Latinos are largely invisible (that is, they appear much less frequently), and when they do appear they are more likely than not to be minor characters.
- In news stories dealing with issues of specific relevance to women and people of color, the protagonists tend to be white, Anglo males.
- Women on screen tend to be depicted in subordinate roles, and Latinos on screen tend to be portrayed in an underclass position.
- Experts, pundits, and positive authorities are predominantly white, Anglo males.
- News stories are mainly focused on events rather than issues. In issue stories, people of color and women are underrepresented.
- Although the research evidence is indirect, working-class and blue-collar individuals (as well as unions and organized labor) tend to be underrepresented in much the same way as women and people of color.

SOCIAL CAPITAL AND THE NEWS

To understand the findings listed in the preceding section, we need to invoke a more comprehensive sociological schema. Although the theory of social capital is still in its formative stages of definition and operationalization, it appears to provide a theoretical structure that explains the sociological significance of the local news media. Although it has its roots in early sociology,[49] the current popularity of the concept was stimulated by Robert Putnam's book, *Bowling Alone: The Collapse and Revival of American Community.*[50]

Social capital is viewed as a resource of communities and is based on trust in institutions and individuals, social participation, cooperation, and mutual aid. Social capital derives from the social norms and institutional processes that enable people to trust one another and work together cooperatively, providing mutual aid and helping with the formation of new groups and social arrangements.

The central theorem of this developing theory is that the greater the social capital in a community, the fewer social pathologies in that community. A growing body of evidence supports this generalization. Considerable research demonstrates that social capital is inversely related to violence and homicide: the greater the social capital, the lower the rates of violence. Galea, Karpati, and Kennedy, using four discrete measures of social capital with data from thirty-two states over the period 1974–1993, found not only a strong negative correlation between social capital and homicide but also that the correlation remained strong regardless of region, urbanization, and level of income.[51] In an even more extensive study, Messner, Baumer, and Rosenfeld reaffirmed that the trust and activism components of social capital are significantly associated with homicide rates.[52] Finally, a team from the World Bank upheld the basic finding between trust and homicide rates in thirty-nine countries from 1980–1994. "Our main conclusion is that . . . the prevalence of trust in community members seems to have a significant and robust effect on reducing the incidence of violent crimes."[53]

In the standard model underlying social capital research, the researcher begins with social capital as an independent variable and investigates its effect on a determinate set of dependent variables, such as expressions of trust in people and authorities, organizational memberships and participation, homicide, and violence. This model has yielded consistent and significant findings. However, the variables determining how that social capital was accumulated and how it is maintained are not part of the standard model.

To use an economic analogy, social capital research is equivalent to studying how an institution invests, accumulates, and spends its money without asking the question, "Where did the money come from in the first place?" Our central concern is in identifying the capital resources of the news media.

The theory of social capital and the research it has generated have clear implications for understanding the sociological functions of news broadcasting and especially local TV news. Our guiding hypothesis is that local TV news programs in their current form mainly function to deplete the social capital of the communities they cover. We conceptualize the news program metaphorically as the mechanism for contributing to or withdrawing from the social capital of the city. Each story is a transaction and, at the end of the broadcast, these transactions sum to an account. We recognize, too, that these transactions can be synergistic. For example, fifteen stories (in twenty minutes) dealing with murder, child molestation, fire, auto accident, and robbery yield something more than a litany of individual instances of crime and catastrophe. They are a depiction of the community as a dangerous place, one in which any stranger can be a realistic threat. To the extent that ethnic minorities, women, and other subordinated categories are associated with these pathologies or are rendered invisible in these transactions, the news program is transmitting a social justification for discrimination.

As sociological auditors, we examine these accounts in keeping with these questions: What is the event making news? What is the territorial base of the event—local community, state, regional, national, or international? What is the social status and role of those portrayed in these events? What is the event-specific status of those on camera—background, major character, authority figure, commentator? Is the event being covered an index crime or a disastrous occurrence? In these events, were those on-camera a witness, participant, victim, or perpetrator? Is the event being covered a governmental or nongovernmental issue? Does the event center on celebrations or holidays or feature a non-news human interest story?

In sum, is this transaction contributing to the social capital of the city? What are the underlying messages about the community presented in the daily local newscast? A story or newscast contributes to the social capital to the degree that it is relevant to the well-being of the community and is egalitarian in its depiction of people by their social characteristics and event-specific status. A story or newscast subtracts from the social capital to the degree to which it is not relevant to the well-being of the community, is nonlocal, downplays issues, and is discriminatory in its selection of persons on camera and the manner in which they are depicted. Examples of news stories that may deplete the social capital of a community include violent crimes, lead poisoning, air pollution, political corruption, police abuse, bankrupt schools, and disruptive city council meetings. Stories displaying positive or celebratory aspects of city life and issues that build a sense of trust and reciprocal behavior include the opening of the city fair, remodeling a regional library, a Good Samaritan rescue of a stranded motorist, or collecting toys at Christmas for poor children.

The pursuit of this line of research has two problems. The first is the problem of apparent circularity. Covering a violent crime story, for example, is not the fabrication of a newscaster. It is presumably the report of an event that happened in the city. Reports on crime may thus be both a response to low social capital and a cause of it. This is a routine problem in social research and is solvable statistically, experimentally, or by longitudinal research. The works of Paxton, Galea and associates, and Subramanian and associates have already addressed the problem.[54] Their work suggests that the magnitude of the effects of social capital on behavior is somewhat greater than the impact of the behaviors on social capital.

The second problem is one of perspective. It is important to reiterate that we are not examining audience effects or the characteristics of the communities in which the news is assembled, although both are critical and important parts of a research agenda. The first step now is to test and document our central hypothesis that local TV news presents a depiction of the community that, in its differential treatment of persons and events, is essentially destructive of its social capital.

In this shifting of levels of analysis, we need to reiterate that we exclude from consideration the intention of producers, reporters, and news directors. Although programs are assembled according to their agenda and news values, as well as structural limitations and financial concerns, our agenda and sociological and social psychological concerns are the view of community that is being broadcast and its implication for social capital.

SUMMARY

Most of the media materials reviewed here have derived from studies of network newscasts and occasionally relevant studies of the print media. Research of local television has not been comprehensive. Further, local studies have focused almost exclusively on the social functions of crime stories, with an emphasis on the discriminatory treatment of African Americans.

The direction of study proposed here is unique from two perspectives. First, the fundamental concern is the degree to which constructed news stories discriminate in their choices of newsworthy subjects. Second, we need to examine the implications of the stories told from the standpoint of the community. In particular, we are concerned with the balance of social capital in these daily news transactions. We will examine this in the next chapter.

NOTES

1. National Advisory Commission on Civil Disorders, Report of the National Advisory Commission on Civil Disorders (Kerner Commission) (New York: Bantam Books, 1968), 389.

2. Ben Bagdikian, *The Media Monopoly*, 9th Edition (Boston: Beacon Press, 2008).

3. James Surowiecki, "All in the Family," *New Yorker*, 16 and 23 June 2003, 76.

4. Robert W. McChesney and John Nichols, "Up in Flames: The Public Revolt Against Monopoly Media," *Nation*, 17 November 2003, 11–14.

5. National Advisory Commission on Civil Disorders, Report of the National Advisory Commission on Civil Disorders (Kerner Commission) (New York: Bantam Books, 1968), 389.

6. C. Campbell, *Race, Myth and the News* (Thousand Oaks, CA: Sage Press, 1995).

7. Noam Chomsky, *Necessary Illusions* (Boston: South End Press, 1989); G. Gerbner, "Television Violence: The Power and the Peril," in *Gender, Race and Class in Media,* eds. G. Dines and J. M. Humez, (Thousand Oaks, CA: Sage Publications, 1995), 547–557; H. Himmelstein, *Television Myth and the American Mind* (New York: Praeger, 1984); N. Postman and S. Powers, *How to Watch TV News* (New York: Penguin, 1992).

8. The Project for Excellence in Journalism, "The State of the News Media 2004," http://www.stateofthemedia.org/2004, 30 November 2006.

9. Gerbner, G., "Television Violence: The Power and the Peril," In *Gender, race and class in media,* edited by G. Dines and J. M. Humez (Thousand Oaks, CA: Sage Publications, 1995), 547–557; G. Gerbner and N. Signorielli, "The World According to Television," *American Demographics* 4.9 (1982), 15–17.

10. D. Graber, *Mass Media and American Politics* (Washington, DC: Congressional Quarterly Press, 1980).

11. T. Chiricos and S. Escholz, "The Racial and Ethnic Typification of Crime and the Criminal Typification of Race and Ethnicity in Local Television News," *Journal of Research in Crime and Delinquency* 39.4 (2002), 415–416.

12. R. Entman, "Representation and Reality in the Portrayal of Blacks on Network Television News," *Journalism Quarterly* 71.3 (1994), 509–520.

13. F. D. Gilliam and S. Iyengar, "Prime Suspects: The Influence of Local Television News on the Viewing Public," *American Journal of Political Science* 44.3 (2000), 560–573.

14. R. Entman, "Representation and Reality in the Portrayal of Blacks on Network Television News," *Journalism Quarterly* 71.3 (1994), 509–520.

15. S. Méndez-Méndez and D. Alverio, "Network Brownout 2003: The Portrayal of Latinos in Network Television News, 2002" (Washington, DC: National Association of Hispanic Journalists, December, 2003).

16. T. Chiricos and S. Escholz, "The Racial and Ethnic Typification of Crime and the Criminal Typification of Race and Ethnicity in Local Television News," *Journal of Research in Crime and Delinquency* 39.4 (2002), 415–416.

17. K. Weibel, *Mirror, Mirror: Images of Women Reflected in Popular Culture* (New York: Anchor Press/Doubleday, 1997).

18. Media Report to Women, "Industry Statistics," 2003, http://www.mediareporttowomen.com/statistics.htm2003, 6 December 2003.

19. I. Howard, "Power Sources," *EXTRA!*, May-June 2002, 11–14.

20. I. Howard, "Power Sources," *EXTRA!*, May-June 2002, 13.

21. Rakow, L., and K. Kranich, "Woman as Sign in Television News," *Journal of Communication* 41 (1991), 8–23.

22. R. Entman, "Representation and Reality in the Portrayal of Blacks on Network Television News," *Journalism Quarterly* 71.3 (1994), 509–520.

23. Rakow, L., and K. Kranich, "Woman as Sign in Television News," *Journal of Communication* 41 (1991), 12.

24. Rakow, L., and K. Kranich, "Woman as Sign in Television News," *Journal of Communication* 41 (1991), 22.

25. D. Graber, *Mass Media and American Politics* (Washington, DC: Congressional Quarterly Press, 1980).

26. The Project for Excellence in Journalism, 30 November 2006.

27. P. Klite, Bardwell, and J. Salzman, "Local TV News Getting Away with Murder," *Press/Politics* 2.2 (1997), 102–112.

28. N. Postman and S. Powers, *How to Watch TV News* (New York: Penguin, 1992).

29. J. H. Lipschultz and M. L. Hilt, "Crime and Local Television News: Dramatic, Breaking and Live from the Scene" (New Jersey: Erlbaum Associates, 2002).

30. P. Klite, Bardwell, and J. Salzman, "Local TV News Getting Away with Murder," *Press/Politics* 2.2 (1997), 108.

31. N. Postman and S. Powers, *How to Watch TV News* (New York: Penguin, 1992).

32. F. Newport and J. Carroll, "Are the News Media Too Liberal?," Princeton, NJ: Gallup Poll, 8 October 2003.

33. Gerbner, G., "Television Violence: The Power and the Peril," In *Gender, Race and Class in Media,* edited by G. Dines and J. M. Humez (Thousand Oaks, CA: Sage Publications, 1995), 547–557.

34. J. H. Lipschultz and M. L. Hilt, "Crime and Local Television News: Dramatic, Breaking and Live from the Scene" (New Jersey: Erlbaum Associates, 2002).

35. R. A. Lind, "The Relevance of Cultural Identity: Relying upon Foundations of Face and Gender as Laypeople Plan a Newscast," *Journalism and Communication Monographs* 3.3 (2001), 113–145.

36. C. Wilson and G. Gutierrez, *Minorities and Media Diversity and the End of Mass Communication* (Beverly Hills: Sage Publications, 1985).

37. Potter, 2003.

38. N. Postman and S. Powers, *How to Watch TV News* (New York: Penguin, 1992).

39. B. Harris, "You Give Us 30 minutes, We'll Give You 289 Commercials," *Z Magazine*, June 1996, 50–53.

40. P. Klite, Bardwell, and J. Salzman, "Local TV News Getting Away with Murder," *Press/Politics* 2.2 (1997), 102–112.

41. The Project for Excellence in Journalism, 30 November 2006.

42. T. Chiricos and S. Escholz, "The Racial and Ethnic Typification of Crime and the Criminal Typification of Race and Ethnicity in Local Television News," *Journal of Research in Crime and Delinquency* 39.4 (2002), 354.

43. On the role of TV modeling social order, see R. Ericson, P. Baranek, and J. Chan, *Representing Order: Crime, Law, and Justice in the News Media* (Toronto: University of Toronto Press, 1991).

44. J. H. Lipschultz and M. L. Hilt, "Crime and Local Television News: Dramatic, Breaking and Live from the Scene" (New Jersey: Erlbaum Associates, 2002), 17.

45. C. Campbell, *Race, Myth and the News* (Thousand Oaks, CA: Sage Press, 1995).

46. Jeffrey Scheuer, *The Sound Bite Society: Television and the American Mind* (New York: Four Walls Eight Windows, 2000).

47. R. Entman, "Representation and Reality in the Portrayal of Blacks on Network Television News," *Journalism Quarterly* 71.3 (1994), 509–520; T. Chiricos and S. Escholz, "The Racial and Ethnic Typification of Crime and the Criminal Typification of Race and Ethnicity in Local Television News," *Journal of Research in Crime and Delinquency* 39.4 (2002), 415–416.

48. W. Hall, III, "Urban Rhythms," *Baltimore City Paper*, 8 July 1998, http://www.citypaper.com/columns, 30 November 2006.

49. A. Portes, "Social Capital: Its Origin and Applications in Modern Sociology," *Annual Review of Sociology* 24 (1998), 1–24.

50. Robert D. Putnam, *Bowling Alone: The Collapse and Revival of American Community* (New York: Simon & Schuster, 2000).

51. S. Galea, A. Karpati, and B. Kennedy, "Social Capital and Violence in the United States, 1974–1993," *Social Science and Medicine* 55 (2002), 1373–1383.

52. S. Messner, E. P. Baumer, and R. Rosenfeld, "Dimensions of Social Capital and Rates of Criminal Homicide," *American Sociological Review* 69.66 (2004), 882–893.

53. D. Lederman, N. Loayza, and A. M. Menèndez, "Violent Crime: Does Social Capital Matter?" *Economic Development and Cultural Change* 50.3 (2002), 509–539.

54. P. Paxton, "Is Social Capital Declining in the United States? A Multiple Indicator Assessment," *American Journal of Sociology* 105.11 (1999), 88–127; Galea, Karpati, and Kennedy, 1373–1383; S. V. Subramanian, K. J. Daniel, I. Kawachi, "Social Trust and Self-Rated Health in U.S. Communities: A Multilevel Analysis," *Journal of Urban Health: Bulletin of the New York Academy of Medicine* 79 (2002), S21–S34.

7

THE DESIGN OF LOCAL TV NEWS
If It's White It's Right

WRITTEN WITH JASON WELLER AND ALLISON EDEN

In this chapter, we focus on the late-evening local newscast. We look at the news story and the manner in which it is shaped by race/ethnicity and gender. This study has four components. We begin by revisiting the basic findings of the research literature with respect to the appearance of persons by their demographic characteristics. We then extend that analysis to look at the structure and content of the news story and how this intersects with race/ethnicity and gender. Third, we look at the portrayal of major characters and authority figures in news stories. And finally, we examine the implications of these portrayals for the social capital manifest by the broadcasts.

Some of the generalizations we formulated in the preceding chapter will be part of the following guiding hypotheses:

- Major characters are predominantly white, Anglo, and male.
- Whites disproportionately appear as major characters in more positive roles. Black males are more likely to be depicted as major characters in criminal roles, especially as suspects or perpetrators of violent crimes.
- Depictions of major characters as authority figures will follow the pattern: white, male, female, black.
- Major characters and positive authorities are predominantly white, Anglo, males.

- Crime and violence are the major content areas of news reports.
- The primary function of TV news is to erode the social capital of the communities in its broadcast area.

DESIGN AND METHODOLOGY

The data to be presented is based on two samples. The primary sample, reported here, comprises thirteen newscasts drawn from twelve cities around the country. The cities and stations represented are Boston (WBZ), Bryan, TX (KRHD), Dayton (WHIO), Denver (KUSA), Fairbanks (KTVF), Grand Rapids, MI (WOTV), Harrisburg (WHP, WGAL), Los Angeles (NBC), Louisville (WLKY), San Francisco (KGO), Tucson (KOLD), and Wilkes Barre, PA (WBRE). Network affiliations included six stations allied with CBS, five with NBC, and two with ABC. The Fox network stations caught up in our sampling were excluded because they are hour-long newscasts and thus not directly comparable.

In each city during a three-week period in early spring of 2005, we recorded a randomly selected thirty-minute, late-news (10 or 11 p.m.) program. Each program was viewed and coded by two and occasionally three coders. The basic unit of analysis was the discrete story, but total times were obtained for sports, weather, and self-promotional advertising. Table 7.1 presents the basic categories for observation and coding.

ON THE AIR

From the opening logo and introduction to the closing banter of the anchors and typically a promo for the station's early morning news show, the average news presentation occupies fourteen minutes and twenty-three seconds. The range was from 11:30 in Fairbanks to 17:40 in Bryan, Texas (located near Texas A & M University, in east central Texas). In that time, news directors squeezed in an average of sixteen stories, with the total number of stories ranging from ten to twenty-three. The typical story was slightly under one minute, although one station in Harrisburg spun stories at half-a-minute each, and San Francisco allocated an average of one and one-quarter minutes to their stories.

This data is not surprising, appearing only slightly higher than in earlier studies with respect to the number of stories and story length. The

TABLE 7.1 The Basic Categories of Observation—Story Characteristics

Story Characteristics
• Story length
• Reported by station reporter, network, independent, weather person, sportscaster, text, anchor
• Race, ethnicity, gender of reporters
• *Story designation:* news, feature, press release, product plug, lottery, stock market, indeterminate, other
• *Location:* city, metro area, state, national, international, other
• *Interactivity:* n/a, URL, address, contact
• *News category:* accident/aftermath, arts, civil unrest, civil trial/lawsuit, consumer, demonstration/protest, disaster/clean up, economic/business, school/education, environment, fire, international relations, health, immigration, labor, media, military/war/terrorism, obituary, prison/prison issues, police, poll, religion, science, sports, technology, transportation, weather as news, other, incomprehensible
• *Entertainment:* holiday/special event, celebrity, features, other
• *Politics–location:* city, county, state, federal, out of state, international
• *Politics–events:* campaign, legislature/legislation, appointments, symbolic, scandal, other
• *Crime:* violent, personal, white-collar, misdemeanors, bias crimes, property offense, criminal justice system, criminal trial, other
• *Crime appearance:* suspect, victim, convicted criminal, witness, suspect's relative/friend, victim's relative/friend, neighbor, police, judge/juror, prosecuting attorney, defense attorney, expert witness, pundit, other

Note: The data for this table and all subsequent tables in this chapter were collected in the spring of 2006 by researchers at the Predjudice Institute.

number of local stories reported ranged across stations from two to sixteen with a median of seven stories.[1]

STAY TUNED

In this section we describe the content categories of the observed stories and their geographic location. We then examine the stories by their race/ethnic and gender populations.

The 335 news stories were coded into the thirty-six categories presented in Table 7.1. The leading categories were crime (15.8 percent), military/war/terrorism (9.6 percent), environment (7.5 percent), accidents and their aftermath (7.2 percent), health (6.6 percent), and education (5.1 percent). All other categories accounted for less than 5 percent each. The third quartile of stories ranged from campaign politics (4.5 percent), sports as news (3.9 percent), economics/business (3.0 percent), and police (3.0 percent).

The location of these stories was not entirely expected. One-third were local and another one-third were national. The low percentage of local stories likely reflected the skill set of reporters and the added costs of enterprise reporting (the independent development or follow-up on stories). National stories, in contrast, were pretaped from the networks. Stories that took place outside the local area or specifically dealt with state issues or state political events amounted to 20 percent. International stories—those not coded as war or military—accounted for 9 percent. There were approximately 4 percent whose locations were undetermined.

There were fifty-six crime stories. Almost half were about violent crimes. Another quarter were stories of criminal trials, and many of these dealt with violent crimes but were coded as a trial when the dominant focus was on the trial itself. Property offenses, personal crimes, and white-collar crimes each appeared 5 percent of the time. Since violent crimes typically account for 2 percent of all crimes nationally, it is clear that this coverage is strongly skewed.

The second most frequent category—military/war/terrorism—dealt exclusively with the Iraqi insurgency and terrorist incidents mainly in the Middle East. Like the crime stories, their focus was on violent acts.

INTRODUCING THE MAJOR CHARACTER

Not everyone who appears on camera is necessary for the story being told. In fact, most appearances are fleeting or accidental. The people caught on camera are basically being used by the reporter or camera person to fill out a story. Of course, there are characters who are the story or are otherwise vital to the story. We established three criteria for defining a major character: He or she appears for seven or more seconds in the story, appears in more than two screen shots, or is the main focus or subject of the story. The basic counts appear in Table 7.2.

TABLE 7.2 Major Characters by Race/Ethnicity and Gender

Race/Ethnicity		Gender		Total
		Male	Female	
White	n	144	48	192
	%	55.6	18.5	74.1
Black	n	36	23	59
	%	13.9	8.9	22.8
Other*	n	4	4	8
	%	2.1	1.0	3.1
Total	n	184	75	259
	%	71.0	29.0	100.0

*Other is 1 Latino, 4 Asian, and 3 unidentified.

As this table clearly shows, Latinos and Asians are virtually invisible. White women are *three times less likely* than men to appear as a major character but twice as likely as black women. In sharp contrast, three-fourths of the major characters are white and seven out of ten are male.

Next we examined the stories in which the major characters were displayed. As can be seen in Table 7.3, almost half the stories (49 percent) deal with crime. While it is apparent from this table that blacks are more likely than whites to be a major character in a crime story (37 percent versus 12 percent), the differences are more dramatic when you look at the focus of the story. Our observational protocol allowed for the dual coding of crime stories (see Table 7.1). These stories were coded by type of crime and by criminal appearance. The latter refers to the reason for the character's appearance in the story. Violent crimes and criminal trials account for three-fourths of the crime stories. We observed that the color of the major characters strongly influences their appearance. Black characters are mainly

Table 7.3 Race of Major Character and the Content of News Stories

| Story Category | Race of Major Character | | | |
| | White | | Black | |
	n	%	n	%
Crime	23	11.9	22	37.3
Military/war/terrorism	21	10.9	0	—
Environment	31	16.1	2	3.4
Accidents and their aftermath	17	8.8	11	18.6
Health	13	6.7	0	—
Education	3	1.6	6	10.2
All other stories	85	44.0	18	30.5

shown as convicted criminals or as suspects in a crime. White characters tend to be victims, witnesses, legal workers such as lawyers, prosecutors, and the like.

Other differences between groups seem less apparent. However, one substantial difference in the military/war/terrorism category, while unexpected, may likely reflect the fact that major characters selected for interviews or shown at press briefings were officers. The absence of black characters may have thus reflected the mutual level of discrimination, that is, mutual between the news reporter or editor and the military. (Military supervisors often limited what embedded reporters could cover and with whom they could speak.)

The time allocated to major characters also reflects the implicit priorities of the reporter. Overall, major characters who were black appeared for 280 seconds, summing across all stations. In sharp contrast, whites captured 2,252 seconds of air time.

SEARCHING FOR AUTHORITY

Depending on deadline, the size of the news hole (the time available to report the story) and the easy availability of a person who is knowledgeable about the event being covered, reporters may craft their story by turning to an authority figure. This occurred approximately one-fourth the time. That is, one out every four major characters was interviewed because they had some specific authority on the matter being reported. We coded four dimensions of authority: giving reassurance, providing an analysis, presenting information, or asserting an oppositional analysis. In addition, we coded authority figure utterances which we agreed were vacuous and without meaning.

Most authority figures (54 percent) were focused on to present information, while 15 percent gave reassurance to the viewers. Paradoxically, given the expert status of the figures, only 14 percent were called on to provide an analysis of the event being covered. Half those, 7 percent, asserted an analysis that could be labeled as critical or in opposition to the dominant interpretation being screened. Finally, another 17 percent fulfilled the stereotype of the TV pundit, namely by making a set of essentially vacuous comments.

The race and gender of these authorities was as expected, predominantly white (86 percent) and predominantly male (seven out of ten). Their distribution is presented in Table 7.4. The selection of persons for expert analysis is a more voluntary decision than interviewing, for example, victims, witnesses, or others directly involved in the event being reported. And that being the

TABLE 7.4 Authority Figures by Race and Gender

Race		Gender		Total
		Male	Female	
White	n	22	9	31
	%	84.6	25.0	86.1
Black	n	4	1	5
	%	11.1	2.8	13.9
Total	n	26	10	36
	%	72.2	27.8	100.0

case, women, black, and other ethnic authorities are either too obscure or scarce in the population, or the selection of white men as experts reflects an unwitting discrimination on the part of the reporter and producer.

SOCIAL CAPITAL: WHERE IT ALL COUNTS

Following the coding of a local news story, judges were required to rate the story on a five-point scale, identifying its value along a continuum of social capital. The instructions for a very negative story read: This story portrays a social problem that may be construed as a malignant property of the city (for example, violent crime, lead poisoning, air pollution, political corruption, police abuse, bankrupt schools, disruptive city council meetings). At the other pole, the story displayed a very positive or celebratory aspect of the city (for example, coverage of the arts festival or city book fair, opening of the farmers' market, the mayor cutting the ribbon at a new wing of the aquarium). Stories were assigned to the intermediate point if their affective tone was basically neutral or indifferent.

There is a core meaning to the concept of social capital. As defined in Chapter 6, *social capital* is viewed as a resource of communities and is based on trust in institutions and individuals, social participation, cooperation, and mutual aid. Social capital derives from the social norms and institutional processes that enable people to trust one another and to work together cooperatively, providing mutual aid as well as the formation of new groups and social arrangements.

The central theorem of this developing theory is that the greater the social capital in a community, the lower the social pathologies in that community. A growing body of evidence supports this generalization.[2]

There were 113 local stories in our sample, amounting to one-third of the stories covered. Categorizing the stories by their polarity, 55 percent were negative, 32 percent were neutral, and 13 percent were positive. Table 7.5 displays the distribution of stories by their assessed social capital. Notable in the table is the dramatic difference between the frequency of very negative and very positive stories, approximately 20 percent versus 2 percent.

There was considerable variation by station, with three stations having no positive stories nine stations with only one positive social capital story, and one station with less than half its stories positive. Negative stories predominated. Overall, the reporting of stories impacting on a locality's so-

TABLE 7.5 Distribution of Social Capital Ratings

Social Capital Ratings	n	%
Very negative	21	19.6
Somewhat negative	38	35.5
Neutral	34	31.8
Somewhat positive	12	11.2
Very positive	2	1.9
Totals	107	100.0

Note: Very negative stories were ranked 1; neutral/indifferent stories were ranked 3; very positive stories ranked 5.

cial capital appeared at a ratio of three negative stories to one positive story.

Gender and race also play a role in the social capital of the newscast. As Table 7.6 indicates, white women are featured in positive social capital stories, with a mean rating of 4.4 on a five-point scale. The other differences by race and gender are quite small, showing only minor variation and tending toward the negative.

TABLE 7.6 Mean Social Capital Rating by Gender and Race of Major Characters

Race and Gender	n	Mean
White male	39	2.3
White female	10	4.4
Black male	22	2.0
Black female	20	2.1

Table 7.7 The Late Evening News—Number and Polarity of Stories

City	Total news stories	News time	Local stories	Social Capital									
				Positive		Neutral		Negative					
				n	Time	n	Time	n	Time				
Boston, MA	13	14:47	5	1	2:24	1	:22	3	5:19
Bryan, TX	17	17:40	4	1	:52	0	0	3	2:27
Dayton, OH	19	15:28	16	2	1:06	3	3:32	11	10:08
Denver, CO	12	14:26	4	1	:25	1	1:00	2	4:33
Fairbanks, AK	10	11:30	4	1	2:09	2	1:25	1	1:44
Grand Rapids, MI	16	15:01	7	1	:28	2	:42	4	6:05
1—Harrisburg, PA	18	15:10	2	1	:54	0	0	1	:35
2—Harrisburg, PA*	23	12:06	11	5	3:39	2	2:17	4	1:14
Los Angeles, CA	15	13:12	9	1	:18	6	5:03	2	1:08
Louisville, KY	22	13:33	9	1	:27	0	0	8	6:30
San Franciso, CA	13	16:48	7	0	0	2	:56	5	7:09
Tucson, AZ	12	13:26	5	0	0	3	4:30	2	1:07
Wilkes Barre, PA	19	13:54	3	0	0	0	0	3	5:14
Means	16	14:23	7	1	0:58	2	1:31	4	4:06

*Note: Two stations in Harrisburg, Pennsylvania, are included merely to show variations within a single city.

When we compare the local and nonlocal news stories by length, we observe an insignificant five-second difference. When we compare their social capital ratings, however, we observe a robust difference. On average, negative stories are presented four times longer (4:06 minutes) than positive stories, as shown in Table 7.7.

Little variation existed in the categories of stories that were local and potentially had an impact on the community's social capital. Of the thirty-six story categories (see Table 7.1), crime stories dominated, accounting for 28 percent of all social capital–relevant stories. These mainly negative stories were followed in frequency by entertainment stories, features of no strong polarity (5.6 per cent), and political events (4.7 per cent).

We turn now to the function of authority in the presentation of social capital. Table 7.8 introduces the six authority roles we scored by the direction of the social capital of the story. It is clear, but surprising, that authority is used to support negative stories. It is as if the story required additional support, especially corroborative information, to bolster its negativity. The mode in the positive stories, "gives reassurance," is also surprising because one might have presumed that the audience was more likely to need reassurance in the negative events. On the other hand, it may be that giving reassurance helps define the story as positive. Nevertheless, what does stand out in Table 7.8 is the overwhelming appearance of authority figures in stories that have a negative value.

TABLE 7.8 Role of Authority in Social Capital–Relevant Stories

Authority provides:	Positive Stories	Neutral	Negative Stories
Reassurance	7	0	2
Analysis	0	0	4
Information	1	4	13
Opposing perspective	0	1	3
Speculation	0	0	2
Uncertain	0	0	1
N	8	5	25
%	21%	13%	66%

SUMMARY

A randomly selected late-evening half-hour newscast was recorded in twelve cities during the early spring of 2005. The study was designed to observe the content of reported news and the race/ethnic and gender composition of the major characters in the newscast. To this end, two observers timed and coded approximately forty variables in 210 stories with a total of 259 major characters.

The following hypotheses extrapolated from past studies guided the research. All were confirmed.

- The major characters, defined in the text, were predominately non-Hispanic white males. The sample included cities with substantial Latino and Asian-Pacific populations, and their absence from the newscast could not be attributed to a demographic bias.
- Whites appeared disproportionately as major characters and in more positive roles.
- Stories that dealt with crime, and violent crimes in particular, were more likely to have black males as their major characters.
- Major characters who were also portrayed as positive authority figures followed the predicted pattern: white, male, female, and black, with whites appearing in more than eight out of ten instances.
- The most frequent story content was crime and violence. A substantial proportion of the local stories were negative. Generally, there were four minutes of negative stories to each minute of positive stories.

Two serendipitous findings, consistent with the predicted results, involved, first, the unique absence of black characters from stories about the ongoing war in Iraq. (This is highlighted by Pentagon estimates that 16–20 percent of recruits are black.)

The second finding, or more precisely set of findings, regards our unique entry into media research—the role of authority in news stories. With regard to the roles of an authority figure, we observed that they were used mainly to provide information or to give reassurance. Further, in only 10 percent of their appearances did authority figures provide an opposing perspective, that is, another side to the story being reported.

The signal findings of this study catalog the polarities of social capital as they are presented in news stories. We argued that a story contributed to positive social capital to the degree to which it was relevant to the well-being of the community and egalitarian in its depiction of people by their social characteristics and event-specific statuses. A news story subtracted from the social capital to the degree to which it was not relevant to the well-being of the community, tended to downplay its social problems, and was discriminatory in its selection of who appeared on camera and the manner in which these people were depicted. This study does not measure the direct impact of these stories on social capital, but our primary assumption is that these stories represent a potential deposit or withdrawal from the community's balance sheet. The discriminatory treatment of characters by their race/ethnicity and gender, the focus on black crime and violence, the emphasis on white males as major characters and as positive authority figures, and the outstanding focus on stories that have negative implications for the community and its citizens all lead to the conclusion that the social capital of the community is being eroded by the routine operation of the news media.

NOTES

1. A *local story* was defined as one that reported a news event within the metropolitan area served by the station. The metro area typically covers a central city and its surrounding counties.

2. *See* Chapter 6 and also Pamela Paxton, "Is Social Capital Declining in the United States? A Multiple Indicator Assessment," *American Journal of Sociology* 105 (1999): 88–127; Alejandro Portes, "Social Capital: Its Origins and Applications in Modern Sociology," *Annual Review of Sociology* 24 (1998): 1–24; Daniel Lederman, Norman Loayza, and Ana Maria Menendez, "Violent Crime: Does Social Capital Matter?" *Economic Development and Cultural Change* 50 (2002): 509–539; Steven Messner, Eric Baumer, and Richard Rosenfeld, "Dimensions of Social Capital and Rates of Criminal Homicide," *American Sociological Review* 69 (2004): 882–903.

PART III

POPULAR CULTURE

8
LESSONS LEARNED

Ordinary people can do terrible things—we all know that—and some of us are scared by the thought. You may remember several years ago when the respected film maker Costa-Gavras produced *Betrayed*, a film about the American right wing. It was panned by reviewers and moviegoers. The overriding critique was that it was unrealistic. Why? Because it treated right-wing extremists as ordinary everyday folk. They were kind to their mothers and loved their children. In the American national character, people who do terrible things are either demonized or declared crazy, and are therefore not capable of decent human behavior.

OKLAHOMA CITY

Although some perpetrators of terrible things are evil and some are crazy, most are not. If we can acknowledge this as our first lesson, we can move on to examine the social implications of Oklahoma City.

The Ethnocentrism of the Media

It was 9:02 Wednesday morning, 19 April 1995, when a rental truck carrying an estimated four thousand pounds of explosives detonated outside the Alfred P. Murrah Federal Building. The blast was felt as far as thirty miles away. When the rubble was cleared, the final count grimly recorded 166 people dead, including 19 children who had been in the second floor daycare center; approximately 400 people were injured.

The news media responded to the event with electronic speed. Even before an investigation could be initiated, news people across the country had identified Middle East terrorists as the perpetrators. They found support for their conclusions from a handful of "counterterrorism experts." As the CNN terrorism consultant—like many of them a former CIA officer—said, "It's clear, I think, that there must have almost certainly to have been a foreign origin to this, and probably one in the Middle East, although, of course, I have no facts to confirm this yet." As one critic commented, "Seldom have so many been so wrong so quickly." The ethnocentrism of the news media was clear in two ways: in the stereotyping of Arabs and other Middle Easterners and in the denial that ordinary Americans could be engaged in terrorist activities.

The ethnocentrism of the news media should be no more surprising to us than was our first lesson. Unfortunately, the media response to this and other recent exposés of its biases makes manifest that the news industry has no self-correcting mechanisms, nor has it any motivation for serious change. The reader or viewer is left with the responsibility for identifying biases and reinterpreting the daily news accordingly.

Meet the Everyday Racist

When it became clear that no foreign cabal had invaded Oklahoma, and as it looked more and more likely that only a few ordinary men were involved, Americans remembered a lesson from their past. That lesson? There is a small, organized, frightening, violent, paranoid, radical right wing in the United States. For a moment the country did a collective double take at the specter and spectacle of the militia, the survivalists, the Klan, the neo-Nazis, and the like. Fortunately for the American psyche, these extremists were a spectacle so they didn't have to be taken too seriously. Look at what they were saying: The United Nations and Jewish bankers are undermining the national sovereignty of the United States; UN helicopters are spying on Americans; road signs have been coded with secret messages to help direct invading troops; plans are underway to monitor civilians by branding them with bar codes and implanting microchips in people's bodies. And finally, the federal government is attempting to disarm the population through gun control—and even by force as the Waco and Ruby Ridge incidents demonstrated.

The focus on the extremists was misguided but not accidental. It was simply another way of saying that ordinary people didn't do this. Mainstream political leadership focused on the right-wing extremists because they are a threat to the status quo. The focus should have been the every-day right winger, that ordinary person who, politically alienated and eco-nomically threatened, has received social support from a circle of people similarly searching for answers and security. This right wing has adopted an American nationalism, a sense of white Christian separatism if not su-periority, and a belief in patriarchy and the reestablishment of a tradi-tional family ideology. The sector of society we need to focus on is the everyday bigot who is the bulwark of discrimination and ethnoviolence. In other words, the everyday racist is the status quo.

The Response to Random Violence Is Random Repression

Peace movements around the world discovered a long time ago that the means to peace had to be nonviolent. On a philosophical level, movement activists argue that means and ends have to be consistent; if peace (mean-ing a nonviolent state of affairs) is your goal, it cannot be achieved by vio-lent means. On a practical level, the peace movement recognized that violence always brought about an increase in the repressive activities of the state, which was inimical to the well-being of all. The right wing, which sees people and society as inescapably violent, views violence as a necessary and consistent means to their ends. Violence, whatever its source, activates an agenda of repression. Within a few days after the Oklahoma City bombing, President Clinton and members of Congress activated their agendas.

The original title was the "Omnibus Counter-terrorism Act of 1995." (It passed with revision in April 1996). Its provisions are likely to do more damage than the bomb that inspired it. Its meaning, capsulized by Gregory Nojeim, the legislative counsel of the American Civil Liberties Union, is: "(1) Individuals and institutions will be subject to harassment and intimi-dation; (2) any alien can be labeled a supporter of terrorism and deported without proper evidence or appeal; (3) legitimate charitable organizations can be intimidated or even shut down at the whim of government officials; and (4) peaceful political activities by Americans will become subject to a legislative chill." While many of the provisions of this bill would probably be found unconstitutional after years of litigation, in the meantime great harm would be done to many people as well as to our fundamental rights of free speech, free association, and due process.

Six years later, we witnessed another bombing—the bombing of the World Trade Center and the Pentagon. And in keeping with the script,

President Bush and the Congress, with record speed, passed the Patriot Act, an even more repressive measure than its predecessor. The news media had by now perfected the art of mass coverage of spectacles, and sociological research had already demonstrated that heavy TV viewers were more ignorant of the facts of these major events than were light viewers and newspaper readers.

We don't need more laws. No one questions the illegality and immorality of the Oklahoma City bombing, and no one seriously argues that this law could have prevented it. We need to be conscious of the fact that people in power invariably use violent acts such as this to further expand the scope of their control.

Write Your Own History—and Other Agendas

There were other agenda items as well, and while they may have come from different political actors, they all seemed derivative of a latent authoritarianism. Some, Mr. Clinton among them, thought this an opportune time to attack "hate radio." Others, mainly media pundits, revived the 1950's catchphrase, "extremists of the left and right." Although no one accused left-wing activists or hate radio of the bombing, the idea of left-wing extremists was (and is) invoked as a neutralizing agent. For example, Suzanne Fields, the nationally syndicated *Washington Times* columnist, disturbed that the bombing was associated with ultraconservative politics, declared that "leftist radicals planted more than 100 bombs on college campuses" during 1968 and 1969. Within months, after the counterterrorism bill had been stalled in Congress, an unidentified "senior administration official" (cited in the *New York Times*) attributed the lack of legislative speed to a cabal of far-right and far-left members of Congress.

Underlying themes in these commentaries link left and right. One is that people are no damn good—a theme that has as its counterpoint the idea that we need to be able to defend ourselves against others. Thus any attempt at gun control would leave us defenseless. Another theme is that our real enemy is the left, and we shouldn't let ourselves be distracted by right-wing excesses. Finally, there is the control agenda, which seems to appeal to people's insecurity—incidents such as the Oklahoma City bombing are beyond the control of people and the only way to deal with them is to increase the power of the police and other law enforcement agents.

Perspective

One of the consequences of such a massive tragedy is that it distracts us from looking beyond the immediate spectacle. For example, a Gallup poll taken for CNN and *USA Today* a week after the bombing found that 39 percent of Americans felt that "the federal government has become so large and powerful it poses an immediate threat to the rights and freedoms of ordinary citizens." Significantly, the poll found essentially no difference in the proportion of liberals and conservatives who expressed this fear. At the trial of those accused, people were once again captured by the grief of survivors who lost their children, friends, and lovers. Americans were fascinated by the psychology of the presumed perpetrators and engrossed by the trial as its reports were televised. These are natural reactions, but we must not let ourselves become absorbed by them. We need to wrench ourselves from the spectacle and reaffirm with others, and to ourselves, the truly significant lessons of Oklahoma City. We cannot prevent random acts of violence by random individuals. However, we can educate ourselves and others so that such acts have no support and cannot be used as an agenda item by demagogues or mainstream politicians.

THE 1992 CIVIC DISORDERS IN LOS ANGELES

The social explosion that occurred in the south central neighborhoods of Los Angeles from 29 April through 2 May 1992 was devastating. As many as fifty-two people died, eight thousand injuries were reported, over twelve thousand people were arrested and jailed, hundreds were deported, and almost all had their lives disrupted. Over one thousand buildings were burned, with more than half that number destroyed, and the estimated financial costs from arson, damage, and theft were placed at $750 to $800 million. This was neither the first nor will it be the last of such upheavals. Our question is: What have we learned from this?

Lesson One: Civil Disorders Are Complex Events

The motives for involvement are mixed. This was not just a commodity riot or a political insurrection. It was both, and much more. There were petty thieves and organized thieves and people who stole food and people who stole luxuries. There were young adults and older ones who engaged in recreational violence and others who engaged in racial violence. It is important to understand not only that the motives of participants and bystanders were mixed but also that people don't behave out of a single motive. Also, motives change over time and in retrospect.

Manifest in these events was a rage against authority, which I think frightened many observers, but we should not confuse this strong antiauthoritarian impulse with a genuine anarchist impulse. These were actions against those in authority, not against the nature of authority.

Lesson Two: Cities Have Changed

The 1965 insurrection in the Watts area of Los Angeles had been highly politicized (which is why I think the term *insurrection* is appropriate). It was confined primarily to the Watts area and almost all the participants were black. The 1992 events were substantially less politicized. While the disruptions spread beyond a single neighborhood, they reflected the new ethnic mix of our cities. Unlike past urban disorders, this was not a black versus white conflict. In Los Angeles, we observed an interethnic melee involving blacks, Anglos, Latinos, and Koreans and other Asian Pacific ethnics. This is the future of ethnoviolence in America.

Lesson Three: The Police

American police have precipitated almost nine out of ten of the major race-related urban disorders. The Los Angeles police, which had been lauded as a model of a disciplined, militarily oriented, high-technology department, have been depicted also as undisciplined, trigger-happy, and likely to use excessive force.

The character of a city's police department is determined by its political elites. In Los Angeles, the elites had clearly decided to use the police as agents for containing its burgeoning population of people of color. For example, the city paid out $8.7 million to settle police brutality suits in 1990. That year, the LAPD had the second highest rate among major city police departments of fatal shootings of civilians. It had been the leading police department in the number of persons killed annually since 1985. In the calculus of elite cost-benefit ratios, the political elites were apparently willing to pay those costs—

and to sacrifice those lives—to contain and control its ghettoized population. (The Los Angeles Sheriff's department is also no slouch as gunslingers, having fatally shot an average of forty-two people a year since 1986.)

Lesson Four: The Political Elites

Racial and ethnic group relations are not on the agenda of the political elites. Following the insurrectionary explosion in Watts in 1965, the Mc-Cone and Koerner Commissions (investigative bodies appointed by the governor of California and the president of the United States, respectively) issued reports that pointed to many of the conditions underlying that disorder. The listing of conditions, which could be the chapter headings for a social problems textbook, included poverty, housing segregation, inadequate housing, employment discrimination, poor educational facilities, inadequate financial and consumer services in the community, and police abuse. In the years that followed, little has been accomplished, if not attempted, to resolve those problems in Watts, in south central Los Angeles, and in the city as a whole. If anything, the economic situation in the city had become worse. For example, between June 1990 and February 1992, the Los Angeles area lost three hundred thousand jobs.

The California Assembly Special Committee on the Los Angeles Crisis concluded, in its report of September 1992, "that the causes of the 1992 unrest were the same as the causes of the unrest of the 1960s, aggravated by a highly visible increasing concentration of wealth at the top of the income scale and a decreasing Federal and State commitment to urban programs serving those at the bottom of the income scale."

Lesson Five: The Courts

Too many people think that the courts are the place to achieve justice. It is especially important for those at the bottom of the socioeconomic hierarchy to believe that there can be a measure of justice in society. And so, even though most Americans felt that the video of the Rodney King beating was sufficient evidence of the guilt of his police assailants, there was a respectful period during which people waited for justice to be done. The explosion that ensued reaffirmed a solid principle of sociological theory: When people no longer feel that there is justice in society, they will rebel.

Lesson Six: Repression

The combined response of the political elites and the police apparatus was repressive; that is, it went beyond the bounds of normal police work. Furthermore, this repression entailed the collaboration of the federal government.

On 30 April, a curfew was declared, allowing the police to arrest anyone out after dark. The curfew was not widely announced nor (according to the ACLU) was it published in Spanish language media, so many people arrested and jailed were unaware that they were violating a curfew. Further, homeless people arrested for curfew violations were, in effect, being jailed for being homeless. Bails were often excessive; arraignments sometimes took as long as seven days; jails were grossly overcrowded; some people were imprisoned for long periods on buses; and people were intimidated into pleading guilty to avoid threatened lengthy detention and potentially severe sentences.

For weeks after the initial disorders, many permits for public protests, demonstrations, and rallies were refused and many peaceful demonstrators were arrested. The decision to grant a permit or to make arrests was often related to the political content of the demonstrations.

The regional American Civil Liberties Union office estimated that 12,545 people had been arrested.

Within two days of the start of events, an estimated one thousand federal agents descended on the area: marshals, Drug Enforcement Administration (DEA) agents, Bureau of Alcohol, Tobacco, and Firearms agents, as well as those from the FBI and the Immigration and Naturalization Services (INS). While the FBI and DEA worked with local police and sheriffs targeting gangs, the LAPD and the Sheriffs department turned over approximately one thousand five hundred people, almost all of whom had been illegally detained, to the INS. Many were undocumented immigrants, but they had not been involved in looting, curfew violations, or other violations relating to the disorders. Hundreds of people were deported, with many signing voluntary deportation orders after being threatened with heavy bail and long prison sentences.

Lesson Seven: It Could Have Been Me

Every person of color, every person who speaks with a non-English accent, every person who has experienced or witnessed aggressive or violent police actions knows that if the police could publicly, viciously beat Mr. King and get away with it, if they could so publicly repress those who protested their actions, then no one is safe.

Lesson Eight: You Can't Effectively Organize Inside a Crisis

Community organizing takes time, and you can't organize to respond to a possible crisis (the aftermath of the verdict in this case) unless an infrastructure of community associations and coalitions already exists. True, small groups were organized and made plans, but the residents of south central Los Angeles were so alienated and organizations so isolated that they could not act in coalition. This is doubtless true of city neighborhoods, especially poorer neighborhoods, all over the country.

Lesson Nine: Denial Is the Major American Response to Ethnoviolence

The events of 29 April to 2 May should have communicated that in communities across America, racism, poverty, and a deliberate policy of political abandonment have created a volatile brew. The fires in Los Angeles spread across the country, with political protests in forty-one American cities, including a major disorder in Las Vegas. Regardless of the attempt of the news media and the political elites to deny it, genuine political grievances and social inequalities need to be redressed. The critical point in the recent history of American urban insurrections is how minority political demands are met. If we gauge the response to the political manifesto of the Los Angeles gangs, the Bloods and the Crips, demands bolstered by their continuing truce and the reduction of local violence, we would have to conclude that no one is listening. (The manifesto, a serious political statement, though surprisingly reformist and nonradical in most of its proposals, called for changes in the physical environment and funding for reforms in education, law enforcement, economic development, and welfare. Among the alternative media, it was described in *The Nation* and reprinted in *Z Magazine*. It did not appear in the mainstream national press.)

Lesson Ten: The News Media Reinforces the Elite Agenda

The establishment news media is intolerant of complexity. Moreover, it tells only those stories that fit the prevailing agenda. Without the connectives or typical embellishments, this was the story they told about the events in Los Angeles:

> Things were bad in south central Los Angeles. The police who brutalized Rodney King were wrong. Rodney King was wrong. The jury acquittal of the police charged in the beating was wrong. The riot was wrong. This was a black riot. The four black men who were televised beating the white truck driver were as wrong as the four cops who were televised beating King. The motive for the riot was really looting. The political rage expressed was all rhetoric. This is what you expect from central city black kids.
>
> There were some good, Christian, law-abiding people in the area. What we need to do is get rid of the bad cops; keep the gangs under control; weed out the violent gang members, the drug dealers, and illegal immigrants; and seed the area with some new buildings, new jobs, and more small business owned by local residents. See? The system works.

Lesson Eleven: Most People of Wealth and Power Believe that the System Works

The country has no commitment to fundamental social change. Don't expect it in south central Los Angeles. The socioeconomic conditions of that area were produced by a confluence of capitalism, authoritarianism, and racism, and these dominant ideologies are unlikely to change. That being the case, much about the area is unlikely to change.

Here are some of the questions we need to ask about the elite proposals for rebuilding Los Angeles. They are pertinent also to Hurricane Katrina (discussed later in this chapter).

- Will the prejudice and institutional forms of discrimination that led to the segregation of this population end?
- Will the level of ethnoviolence that has intimidated the population be dissipated?
- Will new jobs that may come be congruent with the needs of the community and the educational and skill levels of the residents?
- Will new businesses be worker owned and managed or will ownership be from the outside and management along a standard, bureaucratic, authoritarian mode?

- Will real estate belong to the community in land trusts or other cooperative forms or will the land remain as a basis for speculation and profit?
- Will most of the money generated by residents remain in the community or will it continue to be drained by nonresident land owners, banks, and other profiteers?
- Will the police be subject to community control and review or will they remain as an outside army?
- Will the residents be able to effect significant political control over the community?

If the goal of reconstructive efforts is primarily to build new buildings, provide a modicum of new jobs, and finance more minority businesses, it won't work. Our goal has to be to build a new, nonauthoritarian, nonviolent society in the shell of the old. Anything short of that will only recapitulate social conditions that will generate another social upheaval.

THE COLUMBINE HIGH SCHOOL SHOOTINGS

Every major spectacle carries with it the potential of a new way of looking at the past and implications for the future. Usually within a brief period after the event, a consensual explanation is fashioned through the news media and by political pundits, who occupy much of the time that the media dedicates to the event, then become part of the event, and then often become part of the process of transforming an event into a spectacle.

In this case, the event was the murder of thirteen people and wounding of twenty-three at the Columbine High School in Littleton, Colorado, on 20 April 1999. Because of the subsequent suicide of the two teenage perpetrators, observers could only speculate on their motivation. While students were still hiding from the gunmen and while the police were still plotting their strategy, the media coverage began. Perhaps two impulses led to the coverage. First, the victims were not the children of the Hutus or East Timorese or even the Kosovos. These were "our" children and the parents our "friends." Their grief could have been ours. In fact, in just over a month following the attacks, $5 million was donated to the survivors and the victim families, even without a major fund-raising drive.[1]

Second, the event had the earmarks of a media spectacle, that is, by transmogrifying the event to something beyond itself, the news media knew they would be able to maximize their profit margins on the grief and graves of others. Events are news stories; spectacles are dollars. The old TV newsroom characterization of "if it bleeds, it leads" has been replaced in their business office—from graves to the gravy train.

In its societal context, the Columbine school shootings are not an obvious part of a discernible sociological pattern. We know that approximately four thousand five hundred youngsters are killed every year in intentional shootings, with 30 percent probable suicides. That's almost thirteen a day, the same number as were killed in Littleton.[2] The data on all school shootings, according to the Center for Communicable Diseases, indicate that only about 28 percent actually occurred inside the school and that one-third of the victims were not students.[3] For quite some time, we have known that homicide is the second leading cause of teenage deaths. Just the same, counting all deaths among children and teens, only 1 percent are homicides.

Perhaps lesson one is that what went on at Columbine may have been horrible, but it was not unique. Almost immediately following this high school spectacle, an array of stories, many even more bizarre than the Columbine story, surfaced. Here is a sampling.

On 4 May, in Costa Mesa, California, the Associated Press reported that a man who wanted to "execute" children plowed into a day care center with his car, killing two toddlers and injuring five adults.

On 27 May, in Port Huron, Michigan, *USA Today* reported that four middle school students were arrested. They had planned to force their principal to call an assembly and then they were going to massacre those assembled. They had also planned to kill themselves.

On 25 April, in San Marcos, Texas, the *Baltimore Sun* reported that four fourteen-year-olds were arrested for plotting to kill teachers and students in an attack similar to the Colorado shooting. They had a cache of gunpowder and explosive devices.

On 20 May, in Conyers, Georgia, the Associated Press wrote that a fifteen-year-old student in a rural Georgia high school shot and wounded six students. It was believed that he deliberately aimed his salvo below the waist to avoid killing anyone. He was stopped from a suicide attempt by the assistant principal, whom he embraced while repeating, "I'm scared. I'm scared."

On 10 June, in Palm Harbor, Florida, the *Baltimore Sun* reported that a high school social studies teacher showed his class how to make a pipe bomb and where to place it to maximize its impact at the school. The intent of the teacher, presumably, was to demystify the events of the preceding day.

Transforming Events into Spectacles

What gave these events in Littleton, Colorado, national prominence was a combination of geography and technology. Take this as lesson two. Changes in the social organization of the news media, especially the multiplicity of news channels, permit the focus on single events at a level of intensity that earlier forms of news media organization did not. Widely dispersed events, despite their commonality, remain the province of local news channels and newspapers. Similarly, dramatic events that have a short duration and discrete endings—especially if the events move faster than the news media—typically receive token coverage. This is why trials and extended investigations have become the money machines of the media; they permit the transformation of a routine event to a spectacle.

The singular focus on an event by highly skilled producers and newspeople is transformative. The transformative aspect has two consequences; call these lessons three and four. Lesson three is that the level of attention dedicated to the event magnifies its importance. Like moths, Americans fluttered around their TV screens in record numbers. The Columbine shootings meant big audiences. With the story at an end, the audiences tuned out. CNN, MSNBC, CNBC, and the Fox News Channel lost 30 to 42 percent of their viewers in May.[4]

Lesson four is about mainstreaming. For an event to be important, it must be mainstream. Not everything mainstream is important, but the far out, the countercultural, the deviant, or the politically radical is not eligible for membership in the mainstream. Because newspeople believe that they can attract a mass audience only by staying within the mainstream, they narrow what falls within their frames of the acceptable. As a result, only a small segment of existing explanations are framed. Further, given the underlying anti-intellectualism of the media (if not American society in general), careful and deliberative analysis of complex issues is not permitted within the frame. A case in point was the appearance of Professor Jack Levin as a panelist on the evening national cable news–talk show hosted by Geraldo Rivera. Levin, a sociologist who has studied both mass murders and hate crimes, brought considerable expertise to the subject. His sociological analysis, however, was so alien to the host, whose program specializes in the spectacular event, that Rivera "respectfully" declared him "off base" and turned to the other guests, whose analyses were considerably more mainstream.

Another dimension of mainstreaming relates to the definition of the problem. As events are transformed into spectacles, the problem takes on an urgency (also helped by the design of TV news programs) that does not permit the articulation of complex analyses.

Our fifth lesson is a reminder that in American society, if something is broken, somebody broke it. In this event, as in other spectacular events, there was a rush to blame somebody. Although the perpetrators were known, they were not defined as part of an offending category. White, male, violent, and middle class were not categories in the media agenda of blame. There may have been a rush to blame somebody, but these somebodies had to be exceptions. If they were not, clearly we would have to admit to some more basic defect, which brings us to lesson six. If there is intense pressure to find the cause or agent, there is also intense pressure to avoid responsibility. The problem is not me; the problem is you or them or it. Further, your solution cannot extend into my backyard or lifestyle or life.

The Quick Fix

Once it is agreed that something is broken and that it can be fixed without much disturbance to the way things are, it is time to exhibit the solution. With the limitations placed on the definition of the problems, the generated solutions are seldom surprising. Most are old agendas tailored to fit the new spectacle. Sometimes they are downright silly, as when the head of the National Rifle Association declared in response to the shootings that high schools need security guards. The fact that Columbine did have a security guard and that most shootings do not occur inside the school building was irrelevant. From the standpoint of the NRA, this was simply another opportunity to present their agenda in opposition to gun control legislation.

If something is broken, it can be fixed. Lesson eight is that Americans view their world as a model of a machine. It's true for their bodies; it's true for their social theory. Find the part that's out of whack and whack it. In general, this model leads people to focus on a single part (that is, cause). For the Columbine shootings, the list of "parts" needing repair or replacement was unusually long: inattentive parents, violent TV and movies, video games, the Internet, the absence of religion in the schools, the elite treatment of athletes, wearing trench coats, Satanism, the culture of the high schools and, of course, guns. Both President and Mrs. Clinton gave speeches pointing to, as Mrs. Clinton put it, "The culture of violence that infects the lives of our children."[5] The wording carefully points to children at a time when adults were waging twenty-eight wars around the globe and the United States, in particular, was engaged in a massive bombing of Serbia. Government spokespeople seldom refer to acts of the state as "violent."

Too often victims are accused of being instruments of their own oppression. In this case, it was clear: teenagers were out of control, and interventions at high schools were the necessary fix. Of course parents had to be made more accountable, and character education was desirable. (In this context, *character education* is a code for religion.) But the real issue is that by not controlling the high schools correctly, we have permitted tragedies such as this. Lesson nine can be stated as follows: When the elite interests are threatened by the exposure of their role in the victimization of others, controls on the victims are increased. The intended result is to define the public agenda to avoid any examination of social causation. Here are some of the policies seriously proposed in response to the Columbine spectacle: require mesh or transparent book bags; buy two sets of books, one for school and one for home use; establish dress codes, or uniforms, and outlaw the wearing of trench coats; remove lockers; install metal detectors, surveillance cameras, and door buzzers; conduct random searches with trained sniffing dogs; develop profiles of potential troublemakers; install anonymous, toll-free telephone tip lines so students can turn in potential troublemakers; arm principals with chemical sprays or stun guns; and, finally, post the Ten Commandments in classrooms. Of course, enhanced penalties and mandatory sentences for violent teens are on the legislative agenda.

Lesson ten illustrates how spectacular events evoke a sense of urgency and typically arouse the anxiety levels of the audience: It happened to them, it could happen to me. It is not surprising, then, that following such events many propose to increase the level of control: more police, more surveillance, and greater restrictions on privacy and assembly. So not only is there a tendency to shift the burden of guilt to the victims, but the victims need to be protected from themselves. The spectacular event almost always becomes a social justification for increased authoritarianism, and the Littleton shootings were no exception. Two months after the event, the Denver police chief speaking at a conference on school safety stated, "Maybe kids will have to give up some of their individual rights."[6]

There has been no consensus on the "cause" of the events at Columbine. Two Gallup surveys conducted within three weeks of the event are revealing.[7] The first asked youths aged thirteen to seventeen the open-ended question, "In your opinion, why did the shooting tragedy at Columbine High School in Littleton, Colorado, happen?" Four out of ten students focused "on problems of peer relations and peer pressures." They talked of being taunted by other students, being pushed too far and picked on, being made to feel like outcasts, being left out, and feeling lonely. In contrast, only 16 percent of the comments were directed towards the perpetrators and only 4 percent mentioned issues relating to parents.

While the teens looked mainly at the behavior of the students around the perpetrators rather than the shooters themselves, the parents, in a separate adult survey, placed the blame on the parents and families. Only 11 percent of the parents mentioned the perpetrators.

According to the political scientist James Q. Wilson, the parents and the schools are to be held accountable. The schools are there, he wrote in a *New York Times* op-ed article, "to raise good citizens."[8] To Wilson, the absence of such citizenship leads to anarchism—and the parents are presumably to blame for this turn of events. "My guess is that in many middle-class suburbs, parents worry greatly about their children smoking. They just don't worry about them being anarchists."

One Internet pundit shifted the blame to the organized right wing and described the Columbine perpetrators as "adolescent fascists set on a path to destruction by a well-funded international adult movement."[9]

The next two lessons are necessarily embedded in our discussion so far. Lesson eleven is that most people are not well equipped to conduct complex political-sociological analysis. As a result, the analyses presented are typically atheoretical, ungrounded in empirical research, and often without an awareness of their political implications. All people have an implicit theory of society, although their theories are limited by their education and personal experiences. However, this implicit theory enables them to understand and explain reasonably well what is going on around them. Nonetheless, spectacular events are beyond the range of convenience of most of these implicit theories.

Lesson twelve is that American society has a profound anti-intellectual strain, and the mainstreaming of media analysis has contributed strongly to the maintenance of that strain. The role of the intellectual (or professor) is regarded with some ambivalence. One of the consequences of devaluing intellectual or sociological analyses is that social explanations of spectacular events are typically simplistic. Furthermore, the simplistic analysis has its roots in a psychological reductionism; that is, Americans tend to view social problems as having their roots in individual psychology. Instead of looking at the school shootings as a societal issue involving the social organization of the schools, the changing patterns of socialization and the roles of adolescence, the norms of violence, and so on, people tend to look at the psychological characteristics of the participants. The two young shooters at Columbine may have had psychological problems, but not even an understanding of their problems will explain the social phenomena of school and teenage violence in society today.

The Story So Far

Let us review the lessons so far:

- While the events at Columbine High School were unique in time, place, and person, the events and their aftermath had an underlying sociological pattern.
- Changes in the social organization and technology of the communications media led to the facile transformation of Columbine from an event to a spectacle. The consequence of this transformation was to magnify the importance of an event. As a spectacle it commands an audience, and the greater the size of an audience, the greater the spectacularization and the greater the profits of the communications media.
- The causes of a spectacle have to fit an explanation that is easily integrated into mainstream ideas and thoughts.
- Central to mainstreaming is the idea that people, as opposed to institutional structures, are the causal agents of spectacular events.
- In events transformed into spectacles, there is intense pressure to avoid personal responsibility or to accept responsibility for implementing a solution. This personal release enables people to fully become spectators to the event.

- Solutions that point to the culpability of dominant or elite groups, to major institutional practices, or to the class interests of the analysts are not acceptable.
- The dominant though implicit theoretical model of society is a machine model. This model carries with it two basic assumptions: If something is broken it can be fixed, and the fix is usually attributable to a single cause.
- There are strong normative pressures to place some level of responsibility on the victim. Sociologically, this shifts the agenda from looking at societal causes to looking at how the victims were at least partly and individually responsible for their own fate.
- Because events transformed into spectacles create heightened arousal and frequently great anxiety, and because mainstream solutions can neither be self-reflexive nor indict dominant institutions or institutional actors, a strong tendency exists to invoke authoritarian solutions as the solution to the problem being faced.
- The absence of critical analytic skills, or more strongly, the impermissibility of these skills, has several consequences beyond the obvious consequence of sociologically naiveté. Analysts fall back on mainstream, pop-psychological analysis, and media pundits are selected for their celebrity status or their ability to articulate mainstream ideas.
- When serious analysis is introduced, but especially when such analysis does not flow with the mainstream, a strong cultural tendency exists to deny it.

Defining Violence

The same act can be defined and classified in multiple ways. A blow struck in self-defense is regarded by most people as quite different from a blow struck by a predator. Moreover, violence initiated or legitimized by political authority is often not even defined as violence. The columnist Ellen Goodman was virtually alone in the media when she commented, "Over the last weeks, the news has been full of the massacre at Littleton and the bombing of Kosovo—reports that are simultaneous but stunningly disconnected."[10] How can we understand a "culture of violence," she asked, without talking about war? It would be hard to deny that war is violent, but conceptually what links Littleton to Kosovo?

I would ask an additional question. How can we understand a culture of violence without recognizing that most acts of violence are verbal? Insults, name-calling, putdowns, threats, jokes, wisecracks, and stereotypes designed to humiliate serve the same function as physical force. Further, acts of verbal violence can be highly traumatic.[11]

One thing we have learned about violence is that the same social conditions that lead one person to violence have no such effect on another person. Once we decide the problem of classification, that may be the central question for social scientists: Why is it that for two people exposed to the same violent-inducing stimulation, one may act violently and the other not at all? Obviously violence has no single cause, and the influence of any given factor may vary among individuals. For some people the social context may be the strongest factor in violence, while for others the social identity of the target may be the critical dimension. No social factors that we know of inescapably lead to violent behavior. I would argue, however, that the pattern of violence in the American mass media and in public places as well as in families increases the probability of an individual act of violence.

Part of the disinformation that characterizes writing on the subject is the belief that violence is culturally regarded with disapproval. Oddly, few studies have addressed this issue directly. All of those that I have seen indicate that most Americans accept the use of violence to achieve some ends under some conditions. To the extent that some violent behavior is acceptable and possibly normative and modeled in the mass media, people come to include a violent response as an option in their behavioral repertory. This too increases the probability of violent acts.

We need to be clear: Violence and models of violence are part of American society. Violence is learned and becomes, in some persons, a habitual mode of behavior.

The Issue Is Power

When Eric Harris and Dylan Klebold ended their lives, their suicide conveyed the explicit message that in the end they retained power over themselves. Their shooting rampage was an act of retaliatory violence. They saw themselves, more or less correctly, as victims of prejudice-motivated violence. They were stereotyped, discriminated against, and verbally and physically assaulted on a regular basis. They lacked the resources to cope with their situation and perceived the school system and teachers and parents as part of their oppression.

Harris left a suicide note at his home. Although initially reported by the *Rocky Mountain News*, it was too far beyond the mainstream for most news media to report. In his note he wrote:

> By now it's over. . . . Your children who have ridiculed me, who have chosen not to accept me, who have treated me like I am not worth their time are dead. . . . Surely you will try to blame it on the clothes I wear, the music I listen to, or the way I choose to present myself, but no. Do not hide behind my choices.
>
> You need to face that fact that this comes as a result of YOUR CHOICES. . . . You taught these kids not to accept what is different.

Harris and Klebold, armed with guns and bombs, grotesquely mobilized what little power they thought they had. Perhaps at another time or in another place these murders would not have occurred. But right now, the issue is power. That is our final lesson. One Georgia school board member who was obviously aware of the issue said, following the Conyers, Georgia, shooting, "We've got to let these kids know who's in charge of the school."[12]

Violence in all its manifestations is based on an exercise of power. It represents a means to gain power, a way to maintain power, or a response to a threat to one's power. As long as a society maintains the legitimacy of social hierarchies, of the right of some people to have power over others, violence will exist. One can seek either to diffuse the concentration of power or to control violence. By its very character, the attempt to control violence is self-defeating because the control will itself become violent.

KATRINA

Within a week after Katrina's fearsome appearance, most of the basic lessons were clear. This was manifestly another teachable moment. I can discern ten lessons, some more obvious than others, and most point to the political failures of the various layers of government and the ineptitude of the emergency managers. However, the most outstanding feature of the response, and one of the most important lessons, is the way in which people came together to provide mutual aid.

Lesson One: Organizing for Mutual Aid

A day after Katrina touched down, I sat in on a meeting of about twelve people who were committed, dedicated, and fully aware of how to participate in a goal-directed meeting. In two hours they had organized themselves into a task force that was to go out and procure kids' backpacks fully stocked with school and recreational supplies. They were hoping for two thousand backpacks and had already made arrangements for the donation of the use of a truck. This was Sunday night. The truck left with its cargo on Wednesday.

Take some other cases: The director of a private school gave away cartons of relatively new textbooks, school supplies, and recreational materials. "I can always buy more," she told me. MoveOn.org, the liberal-leftist Web site, received donations of one hundred fifty thousand beds. The stories of people mobilizing themselves without grandstanding and in ways that were clearly functional are all over the Web. Its significance, and count this as lesson one, is that we are capable of realizing an anarchist dream: Citizens organizing themselves to provide care and mutual aid for each other.

Lesson Two: Western Culture Has a Conceit of Civilization

We believe not only that we can dominate the natural environment but that somehow we have a right to do so. We should have learned, and maybe some people did, that we need to locate and scale our cities to human and environmentally sound dimensions.

Lesson Three: Katrina's Real Name Is Global Warming

As the environmental writer Ross Gelbspan pointed out in the *Boston Globe*, Katrina's real name is global warming. He reminded us that 2005 began with a two-foot snowfall in Los Angeles, that water levels in the American Midwest, Spain, and Portugal are at record lows, that a lethal heat wave struck Arizona killing twenty people in one week, and that Mumbai was inundated by thirty-seven inches of rain in a single day. The death toll was one thousand, and twenty million people's lives were disrupted. These events, like Katrina, are a consequence of global warming.

Lesson Four: Our Systems of Emergency Response and Rescue Are Amazingly Inept

In the twin towers destruction in New York, rescuers were exposed to a mixture of toxic materials that endangered their lives in some cases and continue to cause ill health in others. In New Orleans many of the rescuers did not know what to do. The USS *Bataan,* for example, loaded with beds and medical supplies, stood offshore for days waiting for orders.

Cuba, recently saluted by the United Nations for its ability to respond to a major hurricane (level five, the same as Katrina), modeled for the world how to deal with such natural disasters. More than one and a half million Cubans were affected and twenty thousand homes were destroyed, but not a single life was lost. People were not herded into stadiums, rescue shelters were staffed by healthcare personnel, and the necessary medical and food supplies were available. The affected Cuban population, by the way, was more than double the size of New Orleans and Baton Rouge.

Lesson Five: The Political Elite Has No Heart

One of the more bizarre justifications of slavery that racialists used to put forward their agenda was that slavery provided Negroes with food and a roof over their heads. The meaning was clear: Slaves were better off under slavery than if they had remained in their home countries. Doubtless, the former first lady Bush, would agree. Commenting on the evacuation of people to the Astrodome, Lady Bush declared that "This was working out very well for them." After all, she said, "they were underprivileged anyway."

The president did cut his vacation short. (He has actually spent almost one full year of his term on vacation.) He then flew over New Orleans on his way back to Washington. The vice-president did not interrupt his vacation, returning on 6 September. As Congress went back in session, Bill Frist, the Senate Majority Leader, placed as the first item on the agenda the repeal of the estate tax. It is important, after all, to keep our priorities clear.

Lesson Six: Crises that Shake the Community Precipitate an Underlying Racism

Racism is bubbling beneath the roily mix of sewage, oil, and toxic chemicals in the waterways of New Orleans. To be poor and black increased the likelihood of being left behind. In terms of housing, it also meant a greater likelihood of living in more environmentally vulnerable areas, that is, close to a levee or a toxic waste site.

Lesson Seven: Capitalism Is Based on Exploitation

Hurricane Andrew, which hit Florida several years ago, exposed the fact that many home builders, contrary to building codes, did not use the proper strapping for their roofs. As a result, countless homes were destroyed because their roofs were blown away. Then, to build on the corruption, the prices of plywood and related building materials skyrocketed. Likewise, Katrina turned out to be the goose that laid the golden egg. Gasoline reached record high prices, and these price increases, I submit, had little to do with mysterious market forces and much to do with the institutional, built-in exploitative operation of the capitalist system. Within a week, the U.S. average price increase was 46 cents a gallon, and Americans spent $10 billion more over the week on energy than they did a year ago in the same week. ExxonMobil alone has been grossing $4.5 million every hour.

Lesson Eight: Centralized, Bureaucratic Organizations Cannot Deal Effectively with Unanticipated and Catastrophic Events

People have hearts and souls; bureaucrats have rules and regulations. First, bureaucracies try to treat everyone the same. ("If I do it for you, I'll have to do it for everyone else.") This may work in routine situations, although I doubt that's so, but it is ineffective in crises. Second, it is the nature of bureaucrats to deny responsibility for their actions. ("I'm just doing my job," or "I'm waiting for orders.")

Lesson Nine: Help Is Political

You might think that in such a desolating event a helping hand would be most welcome, and for most people this would be true. But for the regime of Bush and Cheney only the politically correct may help. Cuban President Fidel Castro offered to send to Houston 1,586 disaster-trained physicians along with twenty-six tons of medical supplies. The White House rejected this generous offer. Similarly, Venezuelan President Hugo Chavez offered cheap gasoline and humanitarian supplies. Because of their proximity, both countries could have provided their assistance in a matter of hours, but both countries have a socialist president. Their politics are clearly more important than helping people in need.

Lesson Ten: We Don't Need More Leaders; We Need Fewer Followers

Leadership in America—corporate or government—is in most instances incompetent. Most Americans know this but don't want to believe it, whether it is a gaggle of corporate comptrollers fictionalizing their accounts; automakers producing giant gas guzzlers; airlines flying people in unlikely directions to fill their hubs; defense industries making armored vests that can't stop bullets; or $100 billion in food wasted annually while millions of people starve. Sure, lots of people are competent, but their presence in high levels of government and industry is slight while the myth of American know-how persists.

For me, the signal event of FEMA's incompetence was the plane load of persons being evacuated who were to be flown to a waiting assembly of helpers in Charleston, South Carolina. The plane, however, landed in Charles Town, West Virginia.

NOTES

1. *Morning Edition*, NPR, 8 June 1999.

2. *Washington Post*, 25 April 1999.

3. *New York Times*, 9 May 1999.

4. *Washington Post*, 7 June 1999.

5. *Washington Post*, 23 April 1999.

6. Associated Press, 20 June 1999.

7. www.gallup.com/poll/releases.

8. James Q. Wilson, *New York Times*, 26 April 1999.

9. G. Hodderson, 19 May 1999.

10. Ellen Goodman, "Casualties Mount in Culture of Violence," *Kitsap Sun*, 25 May 1999, http://m.kitsapsun.com/news/1999/May/25/ellen-goodman-casualties -mount-in-culture-of/.

11. H. J. Ehrlich, B. E. K. Larcom, and R. D. Purvis, "The Traumatic Effects of Ethnoviolence" (Baltimore: The Prejudice Institute, 1994).

12. *New York Times*, 24 May 1999.

9

PREJUDICE AND ETHNOVIOLENCE ON CAMPUS

Although most people view college life in idealized and stereotypical terms, the history of the American college is rancorous and substantially political. Through the end of the nineteenth century, class and religious conflict, as well as conflicts between students and faculty, were commonplace. Few educational reforms came about without major struggle. Then, as now, curriculum and policy reforms resulted from the pressure of students and student movements.[1]

The admission of African American students in the predominately white colleges of the nation was the consequence of the 1950s civil rights movement and court decisions that mandated school desegregation. But not until twenty years later, in the 1970s, were a substantial number of black students enrolled in college.

The early admissions of black students, while socially and sociologically significant, were proportionally small and isolated, providing no immediate impact on the content of the curriculum or underlying educational philosophy. Larger changes in those areas were made later, in the 1960s, through the efforts of the massive student movement. In addition to calls for peace, justice, and social ecology, the movement demanded, and won, a curriculum of greater social relevance and equal treatment for women students. Specialized curricula such as women's studies and black studies provided institutional recognition to "minority" students as they shifted the focus for much scholarly activity.

From a sociological standpoint, the opposition and hostility to the increasing enrollment of black students (and later to Hispanic and Asian

133

Pacific students) were predictable. A rapid shift in the ethnic composition of a population is almost invariably accompanied by increased group conflict.[2]

So, on 12 January 1981, the front-page headline of the *Chronicle of Higher Education* read, "New Outbreak of Cross-Burnings and Racial Slurs Worries Colleges." The story reported ethnoviolent incidents at eight colleges—private, public, elite, and non-elite. (The story could have been written today.) However, the major news media were not ready to put campus ethnoviolence on their agenda, and it was not until the pressure and increasing visibility of events led to a torrent of reports on incidents of cross burnings and physical assaults in the last half of the 1985–1986 academic year.

The mid-1980s were also a time of highly publicized and substantially successful student movements for the divestment of university holdings in U.S. companies doing business in South Africa. However, on many campuses, the shanties that students had erected to dramatize the living conditions of black South Africans became targets for graffiti, arson, and physical destruction. The success of the divestment movement, juxtaposed against the attacks on its campus symbols, points to a central paradox of ethnoviolence on campus: It is in large part a response to the increase in student diversity on campus and to its perceived impact on the dominant paradigms of college education and management.

In 1987, 42 campuses had ethnoviolent incidents that drew substantial media attention. This compares to 103 colleges in 1988 and 113 in 1989. Cases reported in the news media are merely the tip of the iceberg. In the 1992–1993 academic year, a *U.S. News and World Report* survey of five hundred fifty student newspaper editors revealed that 71 percent of the colleges (85 percent for institutions with enrollments over ten thousand) had at least one reported ethnoviolent incident during the school year.[3] Similarly, the Anti-Defamation League, in its annual audit, has reported increases in anti-Jewish incidents on campus every year since 1987. As will be shown later, these estimates are understatements.

What has been happening on college campuses during this period has been happening, in more intense form, throughout the country. Intergroup relations in the United States, as well as in the world, have shifted dramatically since the mid-1980s, becoming more tense, more provocative, and more confusing. Major American corporations, presumed to have reformed their personnel policies, have been charged with failing to hire or promote people of color. Protest activities and civil disorders have followed court decisions perceived as biased in favor of police defendants who assault minority citizens. Persons of Latino appearance or with Hispanic names have been illegally detained and sometimes deported as a result of sweeps and raids by government agents. American Indians, as if in the Old West, have been coercively removed from their homelands and have seen longstanding treaty rights violated. Recent migrants, despite valid documents, have been denied employment. Poor neighborhoods, especially where African Americans are concentrated, have been used for toxic waste dump sites. Intergroup conflicts have surfaced between blacks and Koreans, Christians and Jews, Vietnamese and whites, gays and straights. Gender relations in America have been no less tense or contentious. Increases in rapes and attempted rapes and sexual harassment in the workplace pervade the news of the day.

Although these conflicts are not unique to the last ten years, there are differences today compared with other periods in American history. First, the public and the news media are paying more attention to the conflicts. Second, the conflicts are frequently more violent than in earlier times. Third, a politically sanctioned response to changing minority group status escalated in the 1980s, fostering more open opposition to civil rights and civil liberties than at any time since the beginning of the civil rights movement. This opposition, in turn, stimulated the growth of the Christian right and the resurgence of right-wing, white-supremacist organizations. Fourth, but not the least, is the fact that American "minorities" are more empowered than in earlier times; thus, acts of discrimination and ethnoviolence that might have been overlooked in the past are now being actively opposed.

Such actions, whether on campus or in the larger community, can be easily carried out and condoned in a society where prejudice, discrimination, and ethnoviolence are regarded by many as socially acceptable modes of behavior.

NATURE OF ETHNOVIOLENCE

It is important to distinguish among the three central concepts of this area of inquiry: prejudice, discrimination, and ethnoviolence. *Prejudice* is an attitude toward a category of people. In this context we are talking about a negative, unfavorable attitude, although in some circumstances prejudice is manifest favorably. As an attitude, prejudice is comprised of an interrelated set of beliefs, feelings, and motivations. To say that a person is prejudiced against some group is to say that the person holds a set of beliefs about that group, has an emotional reaction to that group, and is motivated to behave in a certain way toward that group.

There are two further considerations. The first is that prejudice is learned. Because it is often learned early in life, many observers have thought of it as something natural or innate, but it is not. Further, because it is a learned response, it can be unlearned—and it often is. Second, prejudice is not random. For a category of people to become a target of prejudice in a society, a consensus has to be reached that the group is an *acceptable* target. For example, Jews and Muslims are acceptable targets; Methodists and Presbyterians are not. The relationship of groups in society determines the likelihood, the content, and the intensity of prejudice towards a particular group. As group relations change, attitudes change. A large-scale program of attitude change can also affect intergroup relations.

Discrimination is typically described as the behavioral corollary of prejudice. It constitutes actions that deny equal treatment to a category of people. The result is to restrict the opportunities or social rewards available to others while maintaining those opportunities and rewards for one's own membership group.

Ethnoviolence also consists of acts motivated by prejudice. More damaging than discrimination, it is intended to cause physical or psychological harm to persons because of their actual or perceived membership in a group. Ethnoviolence ranges from brutal assaults and arson to everyday expressions of prejudice such as insults, harassment, physical intimidation, graffiti, vandalism, and acts or displays of commonly identified symbols of prejudice or group hatred. Groups typically victimized by ethnoviolence are defined by race, ethnicity, physical characteristics, religion, national origin, or sexual orientation. Gender violence and patterns of sexual harassment overlap with ethnoviolence in those instances where prejudice is central to the actor's motivation.

This chapter reviews the systematic studies of ethnoviolence on campus since I initiated this research in 1986.[4]

STUDY FINDINGS

Methodological Notes

Researchers and policy makers keep falling into numerous methodological sinkholes when devising questionnaires for ethnoviolence research. Asking the right question turns out to be immensely complicated. For example, the following question, which has been used in many surveys, appears straightforward but is not: "Have you experienced racial harassment or discrimination on campus?" The problem with the question is that it encompasses two conceptually separate and distinctive behaviors, *harassment* and *discrimination*. When respondents answer "yes" to that question, it is not known whether they are saying yes to both or to only one; and, if the latter, which one. Even more is wrong with that seemingly clear question. For example, harassment, even broadly construed, is only one form of ethnoviolent behavior. Answers to that question, no matter how assiduously collected, cannot be used to index the level of ethnoviolence on campus.

In fact, we need a series of questions to determine what happened, how often it happened, and what the focus of the incident was (for example, race, ethnicity, or religion). The series should begin by asking: "Have any of the following happened to you on campus for reasons of your race, ethnicity, national origin, religion, sex, sexual orientation, handicap, or illness?" It should be followed by a set of choices—such as called names or insulted, harassed, intimidated, sexually harassed, received insulting phone calls or letters, physically threatened, physically attacked, property damaged—along with questions about the frequency and focus of the incident or incidents.

Such detailed questioning would lead to more precise findings. However, a critical omission would still remain: a time period for victimization. To begin with, these questions evoke more incidents than do time-limited questions. For example, if you ask a second semester freshman and a graduating senior to describe their experiences, you will almost always get more from the senior because the first-year student has only eight months of campus experiences while the senior likely has at least thirty-two months. An additional problem involves time frames. If the population of newcomers is considerably larger than the population of old-timers, the research will understate the prevalence rate. This is true on most large university campuses where freshmen considerably outnumber seniors.

For all these reasons, this chapter focuses on studies that limit their questions to a single school year or other specified time period. Only where comparable data are unavailable are campus lifetime rates used (that is, rates where the question failed to indicate a time period, for example, "since coming to campus . . .").

Most campus studies, including many undertaken in response to incidents of ethnoviolence, are attitude surveys. They measure students' thoughts, feelings, or intentions about matters of intergroup relations. It is instructive to know that 42 percent of the 1993 freshman class nationally considers it "very important" that they help "to promote racial understanding." Moreover, only a relatively small percentage, 14 percent, believes that "racial discrimination is no longer a major problem in the United States." On the other hand, almost two-thirds favor laws "prohibiting homosexual relationships," and one-fourth would confine "married women's activities . . . to home and family."[5] An awareness of people's attitudes can guide curriculum and events planning but is of limited value in understanding campus ethnoviolence.

Finally, in campus research, like any other site-based research, the question of generalizing the findings should be addressed. It is particularly important to do so in campus research because most of the evidence comes from case studies, that is, studies limited to a specific college campus. This chapter cites studies conducted at twenty campuses, although five national surveys, three of which exclusively sampled college students, are included. Thirteen colleges provide the core for the generalizations drawn. Although most of these studies were conducted in the northeast and mid-Atlantic, two factors suggest that their findings are appropriate characterizations of campus ethnoviolence in the United States generally. First, the core studies all used variants of the same questionnaire and their findings were consistent across campuses. Second, there is considerable external validation of specific findings from the core studies in other case studies and national surveys.

General Findings

The most common forms of ethnoviolence are acts of verbal aggression. This is true of incidents occurring in the community and in workplace settings as well as on college campuses. Some of the more reliable and replicated findings from campus surveys are based on similar self-administered questionnaires.[6]

Name calling, insults, and harassment occur with the greatest frequency. Across all categories of incidents and all campuses, it is estimated that the median percentage of students reporting victimization based on prejudice is approximately 16 percent. This figure can be misleading, however, in that the majority of respondents are non-minority white students, the least victimized category of students. At the University of Hawaii, where white students are one-fifth the student body—in contrast to mainland campuses where whites are four-fifths of all students—the overall victimization rate is proportionally greater.

Three observations are pertinent. First, some strong variations exist by campus and by target group. Second, the percentage of ethnic minority students reporting victimization ranges from 12 percent (Jewish students at Rutgers) to 60 percent (Hispanic students at Cortland). These differences may be due in large part to differences in size and visibility of the groups targeted at each campus, as well as to unique situational circumstances. Third, white students display the lowest levels of ethnoviolent encounters, ranging from 5 to 15 percent.

At the University of Hawaii, with its highly diverse ethnic mix, the targets of ethnoviolence are different from those on the mainland and fall into a suggestive pattern. Using only verbal aggression in this analysis, Hippensteele and her associates demonstrated a substantial variation by ethnic group target.[7] Significantly, these frequencies follow the pattern of ethnic stratification in Hawaii, with Japanese and Chinese at the top and Filipinos and Pacific Islanders at the bottom of the class structure. Although the stratification among target groups is different, the findings reflect what is occurring on the campuses of the mainland.

The data indicates that approximately one of every four minority students is victimized for reasons of prejudice at least once during the school year, an estimate consistent with the data of Hurtado and her associates. Based on a subsample of students from a 1991 nationwide survey by the American Council on Education, the researchers found that 32 percent of African American students and 30 percent of Asian American students reported that "they were insulted or threatened by other students," with insults less often directed at Chicanos (10 percent). White students reported insults and threats at a rate of 9 percent.[8]

Findings on Covictimization

An act of ethnoviolence does not have a single victim. Depending on community networks of communication and the extent of mass media exposure, a single act can affect most of a community. A person does not have to be personally attacked to experience the distress of victimization. Here, the term *covictim* describes persons who are aware that others sharing their ethnic identity have been attacked because of that identity and, secondly, have been emotionally affected by it. Covictims may have directly witnessed an ethnoviolent event, or they may have heard about it from the victim or from others. Covictims see attacks on their peers as danger signals to the entire group and as potential threats to their personal well-being.

Potential covictims are the persons who have seen or heard about an ethnoviolent incident. Almost all studies deal with potential covictimization; few asked respondents whether they were affected by their knowledge of the ethnoviolent event. However, in the New York Nine study, where the potential covictimization rate was 30 percent, less than 4 percent of potential covictims said the incident "didn't affect me."

Looking across all students in the University of Maryland Baltimore County (UMBC) study indicates a potential covictimization rate of 48 percent, and the SUNY Cortland study shows 35 percent. These overall rates, however, mask the different rates of awareness and communication among the various ethnic groups. In the UMBC study, 64 percent of black students were potential covictims as were 60 percent of Jewish students. The Hawaii study reports a potential covictimization rate of 50 percent for cases related to race and ethnicity and 43 percent for cases of sex harassment.

These reports of victimization and covictimization form the substructure of group tensions on a campus. The incidents are the basis of stories that are told, retold, distorted, and mythologized. Listeners and storytellers become anxious, withdrawn, and angry.

Findings on Sexual Orientation and Gender Violence

Studies focusing exclusively on prejudice-motivated acts against gay, lesbian, and bisexual students have been conducted at the State University of Pennsylvania; Yale University; Rutgers, the State University of New Jersey; the University of Illinois; Oberlin College; and the University of Massachusetts at Amherst. These surveys have found rates that are typically double those reported for other groups. Methodologically, however, they have not used time-limited questions and are reporting campus lifetime rates. (These rates, as indicated previously, are always higher than school-year rates.) Further, since the size and demographic characteristics of the population are not known, it is difficult to evaluate the adequacy of the samples.

The more precise studies conducted at Towson, Rutgers, Hawaii, and the nine colleges in New York indicate lower rates. The Hawaiian data is 4 percent, the New York Nine is approximately 8 percent, and Rutgers is 39 percent. It does seem, then, that the rates of prejudice-motivated acts against gay, lesbian, and bisexual students are not much different from the rates associated with other groups. Further, as is the case with other group targets, there is a substantial variation by campus.

Studies of gender-based violence on campus (ranging from rape and physical assault to sexual harassment) show a wide range of variation. For example, studies in the 1980s indicate that 30 to 92 percent of women undergraduates reported some form of unwanted sexual attention. Methodological considerations are critical here because much depends on how sexual harassment is conceptualized and how rigorously it is operationalized in the research. Because a defining element of sex harassment is its objectionable emphasis on the sexuality of another person, wide variations by campus may exist due to normative differences in what is defined as objectionable as well as demographic differences in the density of acceptable targets.

Conceptualization of the issues of sex harassment on campus has been taken from laws defining sex harassment in the workplace. Here, two general types of harassment have been articulated. *Quid pro quo* harassment entails an attempt to coerce sexual action in return for escaping punishment or gaining rewards. The basis of the coercion is typically the power held by the harasser to affect the career of the targeted person. *Hostile environment harassment* refers to an organizational environment pervaded by unwanted and offensive behavior of a sexual character, such as repeated references to the victim's physical attributes.

There is a serious problem in adapting these guidelines to the college campus. Many policy makers and researchers, in focusing their concern on unwanted and objectionable sexual behavior, have de-emphasized the broader issues of gender prejudice, discrimination, and their consequences.[9]

Two studies, using different research operations, provide a substantial look at sex harassment on campus. Johnson and Shuman, on the basis of systematic sampling procedures, conducted interviews with 515 full-time women students, focusing on incidents that met three criteria:

- The incident involved conduct of a sexual nature, verbal or physical.
- The conduct was objectionable to its recipient.
- The initiator was a university employee in a position to affect the victim's educational experience, academic record, and/or employment or other opportunities based on educational experience or record.

Each woman was asked about suggestive remarks, jokes, or looks; unwelcome requests for dates; requests or demands to participate in sexual activities; and physically aggressive advances or touching behaviors. Overall, 28 percent of the graduate students and 19 percent of the undergraduates reported having been sexually harassed.[10] In a similar study at the University of Massachusetts at Amherst, Williams found that 16 percent of graduate students and 15 percent of undergraduates were harassed by university staff. Harassment by course instructors was much greater for women graduate students (24 percent) and about the same for undergraduates (16 percent). At U. Mass., where students were also questioned about peer harassment, between 20 and 25 percent of the students reported at least one personal experience.[11] These two studies reported campus lifetime rates.

The Hawaii study, using incidents occurring during a single school year, examined both peer and authority harassment and an expanded set of behaviors. The study systematically sampled classes at the University of Hawaii at Manoa campus, obtaining 926 completed questionnaires from students.[12]

Three summary observations stand out. First, during the course of the school year, women were subjected to a wide range of harassing behaviors. Second, as in the case of racially and ethnically motivated violence, verbally aggressive acts were more frequent than physically aggressive acts. Third, peer harassment was more than twice as frequent as harassment from a person in authority. (For simplicity, the reports of male students are not included here, although they appear in the original report. In both peer and authority categories, men reported harassment at significantly lower rates than women.)

It is clear that sex harassment occurs with substantial frequencies on campus, women are the primary victims, and graduate students are targeted more frequently than undergraduate women.[13]

Findings on the Perpetrators

The central questions here are: Who commits ethnoviolent acts? What are their social and psychological characteristics? When and where do these acts occur? And what immediate situational circumstances evoke this behavior? At this time, these questions can be answered only tentatively, for this is the least understood aspect of campus ethnoviolence.

There are strong indications that perpetrators are more likely than not to be white male students. Also, members of fraternities are overrepresented among known perpetrators. Fraternity houses and dormitories seem to be key sites for violent incidents.

Dormitories are an understandable site given the involuntary nature of intergroup contacts and student inexperience in intergroup settings, coupled with the opportunities for aggression. Fraternities, however, are organizationally active as perpetrators, often socializing their members into elitist, ethnocentric, and sexist values.[14] While most student organizations now embrace intergroup diversity, the data from the Cooperative Institutional Research Program of the American Council on Education, covering 390 institutions, indicates that "participation in a fraternity or sorority among white students is negatively associated with cross-race interaction."[15]

The findings of the Campus Violence Prevention Center's national survey add further to our understanding of the identity of perpetrators. The Center's report indicates that perpetrators of campus crimes (assault, robbery, rape, vandalism, theft, and so on) were more likely to be male athletes and to be fraternity members.[16]

Many acts are not witnessed by the persons victimized. For example, vandalism, graffiti, property damage, and telephone and mail harassment are easily accomplished anonymously. Sometimes the perpetrators are seen but not known or recognized by the victim. In those cases, we can only rely on visible identifiers. One such visible dimension is the number of perpetrators. While victims are almost always alone, perpetrators seem to travel in pairs or larger groups. The UMBC data indicates that two-thirds of assailants acted in groups of two or more. On the New York Nine campuses, the corresponding figure was 57 percent.

On the New York campuses, students were able to identify the status of their victimizers in three out of four instances. The findings are surprising in that more than one-third of the perpetrators were faculty and staff: 21 percent were staff and administrators and 16 percent were faculty. The remaining 63 percent were students. Similar findings were noted in the Hawaii, Towson, and UMBC studies, wherein students cited faculty and staff as perpetrators in 10 to 16 percent of incidents.

Since perpetrators who were spotted but not identified are typically young males, most observers assumed that they were students. However, some direct evidence implicates college-age non-students as perpetrators in a limited number of cases. The first such indication was signaled by two events at urban universities in 1989. At Brooklyn College, three students who were emerging from a Hillel House party early one October morning were severely beaten and injured by a gang that was passing by. At Wayne State in Detroit, during the same month, two men were arrested following two years of systematic attacks and robberies against Chinese students. In a 1994 interview, Grant Ingle, Director of Human Resources, University of Massachusetts at Amherst, described ten ethnoviolent incidents at the University from 1983 through 1993 in which criminal charges were brought:

> In all cases the perpetrators were white, male, and reported to be drinking or drunk. . . . In five of the incidents, the perpetrators were solely non-students, but likely the uninvited or invited guests of our students. In two incidents the perpetrators were one or two students accompanied by a greater number of non-students. In one incident there were equal numbers of student and non-student perpetrators. In the two remaining cases the perpetrators were all students. . . . This can be put in the contexts of much firmer data from our police records that non-students have reliably constituted 50 percent of *all* annual arrests on campus (including traffic violations) during the same time period.

Ingle noted that the University of Massachusetts campus experiences a large weekend influx of several thousand visitors that is generally visible only to those who live or work in the residence halls.

Considerably more study of the perpetrators of ethnoviolent acts is needed. For example, it would be valuable to learn more about the motives propelling these actors—particularly for the design of proactive educational programs. An appropriate program of prejudice reduction must address the motives of actors, recognizing that most acts are a function of multiple motives. Prejudice is manifestly one motive: the targets of such acts are not randomly selected individuals but actual or perceived members of "minority" groups. Acts based on prejudice may also be motivated by other factors. Moreover, acts against minority group members may not necessarily be based primarily on group prejudice. Some ethnoviolent acts may be seen as ends in themselves and others as means to distinctive ends. A classification of motives based on a means-ends relationship is instructive.

Some ethnoviolent acts are *expressive,* that is, they are ends in themselves. This category embraces recreational violence, which are acts committed for thrills, done typically in groups, and likely to involve alcohol. Some ethnoviolent acts are *instrumental* and may be construed as means to particular ends, which may be ideological or responsive. *Ideological acts* are motivated by the political agenda of the actor and their political group. The end in view is to drive the target group from the campus, some activity, or an event, or at the least, to intimidate the target group and minimize its power and influence. A second and integral objective is to affirm the perpetrator's group identity.

The ideological reference groups and sources of identity for these students exist in most communities. Approximately one dozen ultraconservative foundations contributed materially to campus-based programs opposing women's studies, ethnic studies, minority student centers, affirmative action programs, and the various manifestations of multicultural curriculum reforms. Some of these foundations conduct seminars and training programs and offer students internships designed not only for their political education but also to teach organizing skills. The Madison Center for Educational Affairs, for example, subsidizes to some degree seventy-two newspapers and magazines with campus distribution. Although only a relatively small number of students may be members of various far-right organizations and well-versed in their ideology, nevertheless it is likely that most student perpetrators will have dimly incorporated some of those ideological tenets into rationalizations of their behavior.[17]

Responsive acts are not necessarily propelled by organized political theory but are motivated primarily by a sense of threat to the actor's status, territory, or central beliefs. Examples of such perceived threats are women taking over men's jobs, students of color gaining more privileges, qualified white students losing out to less qualified black students, and multiculturalism as an attack on the western intellectual tradition. Sometimes these responsive acts are based on *realistic* threats, that is, on events correctly perceived, but more likely the threats are *unrealistic* projections of threat with no empirical grounding. It is important to distinguish between these two types of responsive acts because they require different interventions. However, whether realistic or unrealistic, the salient fact is that these perceived threats evoke an ethnoviolent response.

A third motivational category is a *collateral response,* which is an ethnoviolent act that is a means to some end unrelated to group prejudice. Typically such acts are committed by students to achieve or maintain peer group acceptance. While some members of the group or its leadership may have targeted a victim on the basis of prejudice, the actors—who may not even share that prejudice—are behaving in conformity to maintain their standing in the group. Acts of violence resulting from group pressure are not uncommon and may even be part of the socialization of new members.

These categories of perpetrators' motivations are presented for three reasons. First, they illustrate the complexity of motivations and emphasize that an ethnoviolent act may have many motivations, although prejudice is always the fulcrum. Second, interventions, whether preventive or in reaction to an incident, must be directed, in part, at the motivations of the perpetrators. Finally, because research here has been so limited, this schema may guide future inquiry.

Findings on Reporting of Incidents

Almost all students who are the targets of prejudice-motivated acts talk to their peers, their friends, and family members. However, relatively few report their victimization to any student affairs office, campus or local police, residence hall advisors, or any other school official. The consequence is that most incidents are not evident to campus managers, even though a majority of a student subcommunity may feel covictimized and intimidated by an incident or series of incidents. For example, as few as 6 percent of the Cortland students and as "many" as 20 percent of the Rutgers students reported what had happened to them. Gay victims at Yale, Rutgers, and Penn State displayed an average reporting rate of 10 percent.[18] The Penn State sexual harassment study yielded a reporting rate of 21 percent.[19] These latter studies are interesting because they are based on lifetime rates and so are presumably higher than a time-limited reporting rate would be.

The most effective way of evaluating these figures is through comparison with the National Crime Survey, a regular household sampling that asks people about criminal victimization and whether they reported the incident to the police.[20] The crime survey data indicate that approximately 40 percent of victims of personal crimes report the incident to the police. The Prejudice Institute, in its national survey of prejudice and violence, replicated the National Crime Survey reporting rate, finding that only 36 percent of its sample reported their victimizations to the police.[21] While these figures are outstandingly low, it appears that college students are even less likely than the general population to report their ethnoviolent victimization.

Students usually give two or more reasons for not reporting incidents to campus officials. A leading reason cited is that the incident was not serious or important. Other, often-cited reasons are centered on the students' perceptions that school officials would or could do nothing. A considerable number of students mention fear of retaliation by the perpetrators or fear that reporting the incident would create more trouble for themselves or more conflicts between groups on campus.

Campus administrators will have to work at creating student confidence in their ability to act and to intervene in the event of retaliation or increased difficulties. Hippensteele and her associates captured many students' experience: "Eleven percent told a university official about their problem, and of that number the vast majority [more than four out of five] reported that this action made no difference."[22]

THE TRAUMA OF ETHNOVIOLENCE

The reality of ethnoviolence is observable in the psychological and physiological stress that people experience and in the degradation of their role performance (as student, worker, spouse, and so on). Recognition of this trauma, however, seems to elude many observers, particularly those who are unlikely victims. For example, an Orange county (California) district attorney refused to prosecute as a hate crime a case in which an estimated 20 to 30 white males assaulted a black teenager, beating him viciously and stabbing him seven times while openly using racial epithets. The D.A. argued that it was simply a case of the victim being in the wrong place at the wrong time and that race was irrelevant. In another example, a dean at a prestigious university labeled a major ethnoviolent incident as a "prank." The so-called prank was the arson of an occupied shanty on campus in which two students were injured. The perpetrators were five white male fraternity students.

Often the social distance between the victim and the person with the authority to respond to the allegation, who is unlikely to be a victim, is so great that the victim is depersonalized; the authority cannot recognize any bonds of identity between them.

Another way in which authorities who are unlikely to be victims fail to understand the reality of ethnoviolence is through "projection." That is, they project their own responses onto the situation. Since the incident is one that they are unlikely to have experienced, they have only a limited basis for an empathetic response. Projecting their own hypothetical reactions to the incident, such authorities are likely to proclaim that the victims are hypersensitive and overreacting.

Finally, observers often focus on the incident rather than the victim. They observe, for example, the expression of insulting stereotypes of students and, focusing on the incident, dismiss it as "just words." If the authorities would focus on the *responses* of the persons who were the objects of stereotyping (and possibly the *intent* of those articulating the stereotypes), their reactions might be quite different.

The critical point of understanding is this: One cannot comprehend a person's response to an act simply by knowing the act. Trauma can be understood only from the standpoint of the victim. It is the victim's personality and past experiences, the immediate situation in which the incident occurs, and the victim's perception of the incident that determine the level of trauma. The same incident that debilitates one person may be of relatively little consequence for another.

Studies of ethnoviolence have examined student trauma in two ways: by asking directly how victims felt about what happened to them and by examining their responses to a standardized checklist of post-traumatic stress symptoms. The UMBC, Penn State, and Hawaii studies suggest, for example, that approximately one-third of victimized students define themselves as being very disturbed by the incident.

One important set of responses of students seems to be avoidance and withdrawal. These reactions include avoiding the perpetrators, changing a major, and avoiding the site where the incident occurred. Students become more fearful of others and protect themselves by withdrawing from campus life. "I try to blend into the backgrounds," said one Chinese American senior woman at UMBC. A black woman, also a UMBC senior, expressed a similar reaction to her encounter with ethnoviolence. "I attend my classes and go straight home. I do not participate in any on-campus activities."

Responses to the stress symptom checklist were also collected in the New York Nine studies. Students were asked, "As a result of this event or events, did any of these things happen to you?" Their summary responses demonstrate that many students were seriously disturbed by their experience of ethnoviolence. Anger, obsession with the incident, increased anxiety (feeling more nervous than usual, and having difficulties sleeping, eating, and concentrating), withdrawal, and impaired interpersonal relationships are the classic symptoms of post-traumatic stress reported by students.

Student reports are consistent with those given by victims of ethnoviolence in community and workplace settings.[23] Further, in these other settings, it has been demonstrated that ethnoviolence victims suffer greater trauma than do victims of comparable types of violence committed for reasons other than prejudice.

DISCUSSION

The new questions raised by these studies, and the gaps and missing information in the data, obviously require attention. Ethnoviolence research can be done at low cost and expeditiously on any college campus. An ethnoviolence audit will not only identify present problems but will serve as a baseline for assessing the effectiveness of future antibias programs.

It will not be immediately possible to evaluate the effects of responses to ethnoviolence on campus. Nevertheless, two central questions must be considered now. What is the best way for university personnel to respond to an incident of ethnoviolence, from the standpoint of reducing trauma for victims and covictims, and of inoculating the campus against a further outbreak? What educational interventions are the most efficacious in reducing the level of prejudice on campus?

Past research has shown that the effects of a college education on intergroup attitudes have generally been positive.[24] Freshman-senior changes indicate a shift away from ethnocentric thinking, a change to greater altruism, a greater acceptance of the equality of men and women, as well as strong shifts towards greater political, racial, and ethnic tolerance. These generalizations are based on Pascarella and Terenzini's comprehensive review of the research from the late 1960s through the late 1980s, which indicated that colleges can have a compelling effect on the attitudes and values of students.

Knowledge that a college education can be a successful agency of attitude and value change has added to an understanding of the findings reported here and should be a sufficient incentive for the design of educational programs addressed specifically to intergroup relations.

SUMMARY

The studies of campus ethnoviolence have yielded considerable insight into the state of group relations on American colleges and universities. Nine substantive findings suggest the following.

Ethnoviolent events, including gender-motivated violence, are a commonplace occurrence on campus.

The patterns of ethnoviolent incidents on campus appear to mirror those in the larger community. The percentage of traditional minority students who are victimized for reasons of race, ethnicity, religion, nationality, and so on, ranges from 25 to 30 percent. The percentage of nonminority white students who are victimized for reasons of prejudice hovers around 10 percent.

Specific incidents cover a range from violent assaults and property damage through name calling and personal threats. The majority of incidents involve forms of verbal aggression, harassment, and intimidation.

Considerable variation exists across campuses in at least three aspects. First, the victim groups vary somewhat; this variation appears to be related to the size and visibility of the groups. Second, the level of potential covictimization within a group varies across campuses, presumably reflecting differences in communication channels within groups on a campus. Third, the reporting and grounds for nonreporting show important campus differences. Although not reporting incidents is the norm, students on some campuses perceive the administration as being less helpful than on other campuses.

Close to half the minority student subpopulation on campus hears of an incident involving one of their peers. Of this number of potential covictims, limited evidence suggests that almost all of them are personally disturbed by the incident.

A substantial number of women are harassed sexually. This is also true for gay and lesbian students. Approximately the same proportion of students is psychologically or physically assaulted because of their gender or sexual orientation as their ethnic background.

The available data on perpetrators of ethnoviolence indicate that the primary offenders are white male students acting in small groups. Although their presence is variable across campuses, white fraternity members appear to be overrepresented among known perpetrators.

There appears to be considerable variation in the identification of faculty and staff as perpetrators. Although they seem more likely to be implicated in sexual harassment incidents, especially involving graduate students, faculty have been identified in at least 10 percent of ethnoviolent incident reports. There is some indication that non-students may be implicated in many incidents occurring at and around public events.

College students are less likely than the general population to report their victimization. The research indicates that, at a minimum, four-fifths of the students who were victimized did not report the incident to any campus official. The reasons given by students for not reporting, aside from their denial of the significance of the incident, were that college officials would or could do nothing. There was also a palpable feeling among students that reporting the incident might create even more problems on campus.

Persons victimized for reasons of prejudice experience significant trauma. Research in other contexts reveals that the level of trauma is greater than in comparable victimizations not motivated by prejudice. Post-traumatic stress symptoms are common among student victims. It is likely that at least one-third of them are unable to adequately fulfill their student role obligations for some time after the event.

NOTES

1. H. L. Horowitz, *Undergraduate Cultures from the End of the Eighteenth Century to the Present* (New York: Knopf, 1988).

2. H. J. Ehrlich, *The Social Psychology of Prejudice* (New York: Wiley, 1973).

3. *U.S. News and World Report*, 19 April 1993.

4. H. J. Ehrlich, F. L. Pincus, and C. Morton, "Ethnoviolence on Campus: The UMBC Study," Institute Report No. 2 (Baltimore: National Institute Against Prejudice and Violence, 1987). The National Institute Against Prejudice and Violence closed in July 1993. Its publications are available from the Prejudice Institute.

5. American Council on Education, "The American Freshman: National Norms for Fall 1993" (Los Angeles: University of California, American Council on Education and the Higher Education Research Institute, 1994).

6. Dutchess Community College, "Survey of Student Perceptions about Campus Atmosphere for Minority Groups and Bias Related Incidents" (Poughkeepsie, NY: Dutchess Community College, Institutional Research Department, 1990); S. K. Hippensteele, M. Chesney-Lind, and R. Veniegas, "On the Basis of . . . : The Changing Face of Harassment and Discrimination in the Academy," paper presented to the American Society of Criminology, 1993; D. Peterson, "Students Speak on Prejudice" (New Brunswick: Rutgers, the State University of New Jersey, Committee to Advance our Common Purposes, 1990); A. Taylor, "Campus Discrimination and Prejudice" (Cortland: State University of New York College at Cortland, 1990).

7. S. K. Hippensteele, M. Chesney-Lind, and R. Veniegas, "On the Basis of . . . : The Changing Face of Harassment and Discrimination in the Academy," paper presented to the American Society of Criminology, 1993.

8. S. Hurtado, E. L. Dey, and J. Treviño. "Exclusion or Self-Segregation? Interaction across Racial/Ethnic Groups on College Campuses," paper presented at the Annual Meeting of the American Educational Research Association, April 1994, 16.

9. The National Conference, "Taking America's Pulse," 1994.

10. M. P. Johnson and S. Shuman, "Sexual Harassment of Students at the Pennsylvania State University" (University Park, PA: Pennsylvania State University, Department of Sociology, 1983).

11. E. Williams, "Sexual Harassment of Women Graduate Students and Sexual Harassment of Undergraduate Women" (Amherst: University of Massachusetts, Student Affairs Research and Information Systems, Project Pulse, 1992).

12. S. K. Hippensteele, M. Chesney-Lind, and R. Veniegas, "On the Basis of . . . : The Changing Face of Harassment and Discrimination in the Academy," paper presented to the American Society of Criminology, 1993.

13. K. McKinney and N. Maroules. "Sexual Harassment," in Sexual Coercion, eds. E. Grauerholz and N. Koralewski (New York: Lexington Books, 1991).

14. P. Y. Martin, and R. A. Hummer, "Fraternities and Rape on Campus," *Gender and Society* 3 (1989), 457–473; P. R. Sanday, *Sex, Brotherhood, and Privilege on Campus* (New York: New York University Press, 1991).

15. S. Hurtado, E. L. Dey, and J. Treviño. "Exclusion or Self-Segregation? Interaction across Racial/Ethnic Groups on College Campuses," paper presented at the Annual Meeting of the American Educational Research Association, April 1994, 21.

16. R. B. Bausell, C. R. Bausell, and D. G. Siegel, "The Links Among Alcohol, Drugs and Crime on American College Campuses: A National Follow-Up Study" (Towson, MD: Towson State University, Campus Violence Prevention Center, 1991).

17. D. Massachi and R. Cowan, "Uncovering the Right on Campus" (Cambridge, MA: University Conversion Project, 1994).

18. K. T. Berrill, "Anti-Gay Violence and Victimization in the United States: An Overview" in *Hate Crimes: Confronting Violence against Lesbians and Gay Men*, eds. G. M. Herek and K. T. Berrill (Newberry Park, CA: Sage, 1992).

19. M. P. Johnson and S. Shuman, "Sexual Harassment of Students at the Pennsylvania State University" (University Park, PA: Pennsylvania State University, Department of Sociology, 1983).

20. Justice Statistics Clearinghouse (Washington, DC: U.S. Department of Justice, Bureau of Justice Statistics, 1994).

21. H. J. Ehrlich, "The Ethnoviolence Project" (Baltimore: National Institute Against Prejudice and Violence, 1992). The National Institute Against Prejudice and Violence closed in July 1993. Its publications are available from the Prejudice Institute.

22. S. K. Hippensteele, M. Chesney-Lind, and R. Veniegas, "On the Basis of . . . : The Changing Face of Harassment and Discrimination in the Academy," paper presented to the American Society of Criminology, 1993.

23. H. J. Ehrlich, B. E. K. Larcom, and R. D. Purvis. "The Traumatic Effects of Ethnoviolence" (Baltimore: the Prejudice Institute, 1994).

24. E. T. Pascarella and P. T. Terenzini, *How College Affects Students* (San Francisco: Jossey-Bass, 1991).

PART IV

THE STRUGGLE CONTINUES

10

PROFILING THE BELIEF
STRUCTURE OF RIGHT-WING GROUPS

I prepared the checklist in this chapter as a means of assisting students in analyzing right-wing groups along the spectrum from conservatives to racial supremacists to neofascists.

Students have to learn how to go about making observations from the standpoint of a detached social scientist. This checklist, first of all, helps guide their observations. Second, the application of the checklist to a particular group or groups constrains students to think about their own position on the various items in the checklist. At this point, the teacher can help students comprehend the reflexive character of social inquiry.

The checklist serves another function. People tend to react emotionally to right-wing groups—to ridicule them and pull away in revulsion. The checklist keeps them on course and reduces the observers' tendency to stereotype these groups.

Underlying the development of this checklist is a rejection of the simplistic, unidimensional models that characterize much discourse in this arena. Typically these models move along a postulated continuum from right to left or from conservative to liberal. Even though they are in vogue, most people seem to find the models confusing and inadequate in describing these complex ideologies. My hope is that this checklist can unfold these layers of complexity and help the observer better comprehend the belief structures that make up the right wing. I present these items by topical area, and it may be helpful to visualize a particular group as you go through the checklist.

RACE

- ❏ Believes that race is a determinant of behavior and culture.
- ❏ Believes that one's own race/ethnicity should be valued more than any other.
- ❏ May display a racial ethnocentrism, that is, may glorify one's own race while denigrating others (or may present only a preference without a clear articulation of a complete ethnocentric statement).
- ❏ May present a fear of ethnic nationalist movements.
- ❏ May present a belief in a racial/ethnic hierarchy or a direct statement of genetic superiority/inferiority.
- ❏ Believes that blacks and whites cannot live together. This separatism may be presented across a range of beliefs from advocating genocide or segregation or deportation. This separatism extends to all non-Aryans.
- ❏ Believes that the mixing of races and cultures weakens the white race and culture.
- ❏ Believes that the white working class is shrinking and endangered.

GENDER

- ❏ Believes that gender determines behavior and that males should be dominant.
- ❏ Believes that a woman's primary function is mothering and that the optimum context for this is in the traditional nuclear family.
- ❏ Believes that abortion is a usurpation of the female role and may also be against God's will.
- ❏ May believe that working outside the home has a destructive effect on the traditional family.
- ❏ Believes that men are the breadwinners and women are the homemakers.
- ❏ Believes that the ERA and other attempts to assert gender equality must be opposed.

THE JEWISH CONSPIRACY

- ❏ Believes that Jews are evil and responsible for most existing social problems. This may be presented in multiple beliefs.

❑ At a religious level, may regard Jews as the killers of Christ, as the offspring of Satan, or as usurpers of the true chosen people, namely Aryans.

❑ At a political level, may regard Jews as predominately liberal or communist or both, as the controllers of the government, as the owners of mass media, and as the bankers and international financiers.

❑ May present a variety of beliefs that Jews kidnap and sacrifice young children.

❑ Believes that the Holocaust never happened or happened in numbers that were consonant with normal warfare.

❑ May present the related belief that Hitler and the Nazis weren't so bad and that the Holocaust is Jewish propaganda designed to discredit Hitler and maintain support for Israel.

RELIGION

❑ Believes that the United States was begun as a Christian nation (and that the Supreme Court has upheld that principle).

❑ Believes in a revisionist Christianity that views Aryans as the chosen people, Jews as the offspring of Satan, and nonwhites as pre-Adamic, that is, God's mistake.

❑ Believes that there is no constitutional requirement for the separation of church and state, and that the separation of church and state has created an amoral if not immoral secular nation.

❑ May promote Christian symbolism, especially in schools: periods of religious silence, display of the Ten Commandments, teaching of creationism, Christmas displays of the Nativity scene.

SEXUAL ORIENTATION

❑ Believes that homosexuality is contrary to God's will, immoral, and illegal.

❑ May construe AIDS as divine punishment for homosexuality.

❑ May present a belief that gay men are child molesters.

POLITICS AND COMMUNITY

❑ Politically, there is a romanticization of community (presumably in a time past) and a fear of those forces that are seen as destroying or decreasing the possibility of community.

❑ Believes that crime is increasing and can be controlled only by adopting a more punitive attitude toward criminals, including building more prisons and control units, mandating longer sentences, decreasing parole, and maintaining capital punishment.

❑ Believes that violence is a justifiable means for maintaining American power in the world.

❑ Believes that a political struggle is underway and many of the forces of the world are already involved in destroying the white working class.

❑ May believe that the U.S. government has already been taken over (Zionist Occupational Government, ZOG) and international forces are already at work within these borders.

❑ Believes that communists, socialists, and (these days) liberals are enemies of the American state.

❑ May believe that the various programs of public assistance, such as AFDC, food stamps, minimum wage, school desegregation, affirmative action, and minority set-asides are mainly techniques for weakening a white power base.

EDUCATION OF CHILDREN
(ELEMENTARY AND SECONDARY)

❑ Opposes teaching critical of America.

❑ Opposes the demythologizing of Columbus and the discovery of America.

❑ Opposes the expansion of multicultural themes within the curriculum.

❑ Opposes sex education, including information about and the distribution of birth control methods.

❑ Opposes teaching about alternatives to the nuclear family.

❑ Opposes values education.

❑ Opposes efforts to desegregate schools, including busing.

❑ May believe that the absence of school prayer is central to violence in the schools and declining student performance.

❏ Wants to reinstitute school prayers.
❏ Wants to institute curricular changes that would:
    ❏ Sustain America, American values, and Christian values.
    ❏ Advance the sacredness of the nuclear family and so-called family values.
    ❏ Teach the harm of premarital sex and the use of birth control devices.
    ❏ Teach creationism or intelligent design as a scientific challenge to evolutionary theory.
❏ Wants to develop a system of school vouchers to avoid "problems" in the public school systems.

THE UNIVERSITY

❏ Believes that most universities are breeding grounds for the subversion of American society.
❏ Opposes speech codes and codes of conduct.
❏ Opposes multicultural curricular reforms.
❏ Opposes political correctness.
❏ Opposes ethnic and women's studies.
❏ Opposes the recognition of lesbians, gays, and bisexuals as eligible student organizations or as entitled to inclusion in civil rights codes.
❏ Opposes the recognition of the Holocaust.
❏ Opposes affirmative action and minority recruitment.
❏ Opposes radical or deviant or liberal faculty.
❏ Opposes concerns with sex harassment.

WORLD VIEW

❏ The general world view of the far right is that the world is a jungle, a dangerous place, populated by people who are naturally (and if left unchecked by social forces) selfish and evil. In this context, there is a need for strict controls, punishment, and capital punishment.
❏ They believe that current social problems in society have their origins in the pathology of black culture, the influx of immigrants, and the social policies that have been developed to ameliorate the social position of blacks, Hispanics, Asians, and women.

STRATEGY FOR POLITICAL SOCIAL CHANGE

The far-right agrees on the need for fundamental social structural changes. No apparent consensus exists with regard to aggressive armed struggle as the means for revolutionary change and the overthrow of the existing U.S. government. There does seem to be a variety of strategic visions, including an impending apocalypse that will take the form of a nuclear war or a race war and a vision of building a secessionist movement that will carve out ethnic pockets for the people of the United States.

CODA

Chris Hedges, former reporter at the *New York Times,* summarizes the violence of the right-wing program:

> All debates with the Christian Right are useless. We cannot reach this movement. It does not want a dialogue. It cares nothing for rational thought and discussion. It is not mollified because John Kerry prays or Jimmy Carter teaches Sunday School. These naive attempts to reach out to a movement bent on our destruction, to prove to them that we too have "values," would be humorous if the stakes were not so deadly. They hate us. They hate the liberal, enlightened world formed by the Constitution. Our opinions do not count.
>
> This movement will not stop until we are ruled by Biblical Law, an authoritarian church intrudes in every aspect of our life, women stay at home and rear children, gays agree to be cured, abortion is considered murder, the press and the schools promote "positive" Christian values, the federal government is gutted, war becomes our primary form of communication with the rest of the world and recalcitrant non-believers see their flesh eviscerated at the sound of the Messiah's voice.[1]

NOTES

1. Chris Hedges, "The Christian Right and the Rise of American Facism," *Theocracy Watch*, http://www.theocracywatch.org/chris_hedges_nov24_04.htm, 15 November 2004.

11

A BRIEF NOTE ON THE POLITICS OF IGNORANCE

Let's be clear: ignorance is not the same as stupidity. And ignorance is not the same as political ignorance. A survey of Americans found that 48 percent believe that oatmeal is made from wheat. More than one-quarter do not know that the earth revolves around the sun. This sort of ignorance is accompanied by a startling array of mystical and mythical beliefs. Of those who participated in a 2006 Gallup Halloween survey, 48 percent said they believed in ghosts and, in a *Washington Post* study, one-fourth stated their belief that "aliens from outer space are living here on Earth right now." In the realm of religious practice, pollsters find that more than eight out of ten believe in miracles and more than half believe that they have experienced or witnessed one. In a May 2004 Gallup sample, 70 percent said they believe in the devil and 10 percent said they were not sure. Although these beliefs may have consequences for peoples' political behavior, this is not our concern.

Political ignorance *is* our concern. It has four attributes. It is shared; that is, many people hold the beliefs and information in common—share it, and teach it to others. Second, what they hold in common are beliefs that have a direct implication for the distribution of wealth and privilege in society. Third, the information they share is false or misleading. Finally, this information distracts people from autonomous and democratic behavior. The media analyst Neil Postman writes of this as creating an "illusion of knowing something but which in fact leads one away from knowing."

Consider the implications of the following survey results. In 1991, two out of three Americans did not know that the Bill of Rights is the first ten amendments to the Constitution.[1] One-fifth thought it referred to any law passed by Congress dealing with rights. Moreover, in another survey, one-fifth of the people indicated the belief that the president can suspend the Bill of Rights during war time.[2] And one out of six believes that the Constitution established the United States as a Christian nation.

A majority of the American public (60 percent) can't answer basic questions about our economic system. And while crime and personal security may be central concerns, most of the legislation that seems to have public support is based on unsupported and sometimes false assumptions about crime, drug use, imprisonment, recidivism, and violence.

The magnitude of clear political ignorance requires an intensive look. The political scientist Stephen Bennett studied political ideology by analyzing data collected in the University of Michigan's voter surveys in 1984, 1988, and 1992. His analysis indicated that two-thirds of Americans had little understanding of the meaning of conservative and liberal. In all of those presidential elections, close to half of those interviewed could not distinguish which of the candidates was the more conservative or liberal: Reagan versus Mondale, Bush versus Dukakis, or Clinton versus Bush.[3] The researcher concluded that about one-third of all Americans had little understanding of the meaning of liberalism and conservatism. Only 6 percent of eighth graders understand the function of a constitution. Most lacked any understanding of how government works.[4]

The *Washington Post*'s former polling editor has argued that evidence suggests that younger people today are more politically ignorant than their age mates of 1941–1975 and that the turning point occurred in the mid-1970s and is continuing.[5]

American political history seems to have eluded a staggering proportion of teenagers and young adults. One in five teenagers did not know who the colonists fought in the Revolutionary War. One in four did not know who fought in the Civil War (13 percent thought the war was between the United States and England). Is it surprising then that 63 percent of Americans ages eighteen to twenty-four cannot locate Iraq on a world map?

Political ignorance is manifest especially in the beliefs that white Americans hold about the position of blacks in society. Whites perceive the black population at about twice the size it actually is. Two out of five whites believe that there is no serious discrimination in society; that is, they believe blacks are treated equally or the same as whites. Moreover, in repeated surveys, a majority of whites indicate their belief that blacks have achieved equal opportunity in education, health care, housing, employment, and income.[6]

Community conflicts, such as those over the teaching of evolution, may best be understood by the deep level of ignorance characterizing the dispute. For example, only 10 percent of American adults believe in evolution (as compared to a belief in creationism or in intelligent design). This percentage has been constant over the past twenty years.[7]

People are politically ignorant because their socialization and social pressure have guided them to that state. Few people set out to be misinformed, although some find a certain comfort in ignoring the discomforts of others. The major social function of political ignorance is to decrease the likelihood of dissent. As a mechanism of oppression it is most successful when it obscures political understanding from those who are themselves the victims of social injustice.

As a tool of oppression, political ignorance insulates people from the obscenities of capitalism, racism and sexism, and the concentration of power in society. Even more, it insulates people from those of us engaged in political education.

NOTES

1. American Bar Association, 1991.

2. "Harper's Index," *Harper's Magazine,* July 1992.

3. *Washington Post,* 29 January 1995.

4. National Assessment for Educational Progress, 1998.

5. *Washington Post, National Weekly Edition,* 9–15 July 1990.

6. Valene Whittaker and Howard Ehrlich, "In the Eyes of the Beholder," *Perspectives* (2001), n. 21–22.

7. Deborah Carr, "Monkeying with Science," *Context* (Spring 2006), 50.

12

STEP BY STEP
A Personal Trek

It would be myopic not to see that our society is so irrational that
its most fundamental premises must be challenged. I refer to
the problem of mindless economic growth, massive social inequities,
widespread public disempowerment, and an almost apocalyptic
clash between humanity and the natural world.

MURRAY BOOKCHIN

We opened this book with a Cherokee maxim that declared that if we continued along this path, we shall get to where we are going. In this chapter, I want to take us off this path, step by step. This is where I am going.

STEP ONE

At the end of 2006, twenty-six major wars were ongoing in the world. (A major war is defined as one in which more than one thousand people have been killed.) With few exceptions, all have been motivated by race, ethnicity, religion, or nationality. All these wars are historically unique but sociologically patterned. Our studies offer no path to peace. There is none. Peace is the way. How, then, do we track our journey?

STEP TWO

It is my perspective that the role of the social scientist is to formulate a view of a good society and to test hypotheses that validate or invalidate that view as well as test our ideas of the best social policies. Much of our work is descriptive. It differs from journalism in that our methodology, including our insistence on replication, is far more demanding. As social scientists, we must maintain that rigor while retaining a focus on sketching the outlines of a new society. This is not meant to be a blueprint of a utopian community. That's why I talk of "hypotheses" derived from our sketch. For example, our new society would likely allow people to live wherever they chose. But what does that mean with regard to class, age, and position in the life cycle as well as accessibility of work and school? There are more questions, of course, and the answers must be asserted tentatively and be testable.

STEP THREE

In our advocacy for social and economic justice, we need to recognize that there is no elite commitment to such a radical change. There is no resolve among the political, business, educational, or religious leaders regarding principles of social justice or an equitable economy. This is not to say that no elites will walk with us; just that few will forgo their privileged position. Much of the middle class will drift in whatever direction the political currents take them.

STEP FOUR

While our objectives are changes in social structure, we need to keep in mind the psychological consequences of oppression that deter us from positive action. Gustav Landauer, an early twentieth-century anarchist philosopher, reminded his readers: "The state is in our head." The intersection of rapid changes in the society and a culture of denial leads people not only to fear change but to deny that change is necessary or desirable. However, even when people come to perceive that the system is unjust and then embrace change and are willing to act, they don't necessarily know what to do. This itself can lead to inaction.

That first step is often isolating, at least to begin with, because the actor has to develop a new reference group, a step that often isolates people from their significant others. There is a price to be paid for social activism, and people have to be convinced that their new goals are attainable, even though the changes may be in the far future, and they have to feel that society will be better off in the future.

STEP FIVE

The starting point in our political practice is our view of a good society. What is it we seek? I reiterate: we do not need nor should we pursue a blueprint. It is sufficient, for example, to extend a view of a participatory democracy without necessarily resolving all the detailed problems that such as view entails. And it may turn out, as I believe it will, that as we try to work out the details we will reshape our view.

Often, our sketch begins with erasing the slate on which we were drawing. For example, we can hold out the vision of the absence of war without knowing fully what a world at peace would necessarily look like.

My own view, fashioned by my work in race and ethnic relations, comprises three dimensions: freedom from coercion, a participatory democracy, and a participatory economy. Furthermore, my sketch has no room for a capitalist economy. Such an economy is necessarily coercive, undemocratic, and fails to provide the goods and services in society at a level of need.

STEP SIX

In our struggles, means and ends need to be consistent. Although this sounds like a parental scold, it is a truly radical demand. In fact, I believe the failure of our practice of democracy is in large measure due to our failure to practice democracy in our everyday behavior. As a society we lay claim to democracy in the realm of government and politics. But we dismiss the ideas of a democratic workplace, a democratic school, a democratic city economy, and so on. Unless the groups in which we participate conduct their affairs in a nonauthoritarian, democratic fashion, a democratic government cannot be realized. Authoritarianism is preserved by the compartmentalization of democracy.

STEP SEVEN

Most people confuse democracy with one person, one vote. Genuine democracy is best understood as a complex organizational form that facilitates a decision-making structure designed to minimize power differentials and optimize self-management and mutual aid. In her mockingly titled book, *Freedom Is an Endless Meeting*, Francesca Polletta sketches the basis of a participatory democracy which she describes as

> a macropolitical vision of political and economic institutions governed by their constituents, an organizational form characterized by decentralization, a minimal division of labor, and an egalitarian ethos, and a mode of decision-making that is direct rather than representative and relies on consensus rather than majority rule.[1]

Robin Hahnel, in his book *Economic Justice and Democracy*, writes that to achieve social justice in society, we will need to meld participatory democracy with a participatory economy. He reminds us that "any system of economic cooperation that does not benefit people equally is not treating people as equals."[2]

STEP EIGHT

Building an egalitarian ethos requires a normative structure of intergroup and interpersonal relations. A constitution, at one level, or a set of organizational bylaws, at another level, are examples of codified norms that articulate what is and is not acceptable. The fact that we have such norms does not mean that they will be acted upon. The history of civil rights laws is a case in point. Nevertheless, a normative structure supporting egalitarian relations is a necessary condition of such relations.

STEP NINE

The counterarguments to participation in decision-making take numerous forms, although a rejection of equality is at the root of these arguments. Perhaps the most common rejection of participatory democracy has been labeled by some as the "realist theory of democracy." This is the belief that the highest form of democracy is one in which only those who are most knowledgeable take part in making important decisions. Thus, many realist theorists regard "get out the vote drives" as counterproductive because they will likely mobilize the uninformed. This line of thought is at the heart of the older exclusionist norms that barred from voting, at various time, blacks, women, non-Christians, and persons who did not own property.

A different argument, and one that is most common today, is the critique of the decision-making process itself. Rather than identify people's inability to make informed decisions, this critique focuses on process. It often begins by identifying the process as coercive. Participation is viewed as obligatory, when in practice it is taken as an ideal norm. Moreover, because not all decisions affect all people, participation is pragmatically and voluntarily limited to those who are concerned by the decision.

STEP TEN

The fact of decisional equality disturbs other critics who see the process as ignoring or running roughshod over the different talents and skills that people bring to a meeting. These critics appear to be concerned that persons with authoritative knowledge might be ignored in the decision process and the process will likely lead to the wrong decision. To unravel this argument, we need to distinguish between being *an* authority and being *in* authority. An authority is presumably a person who possesses greater knowledge of a particular matter than others because of experience, training, study, and so on. Being in authority means that the person has the power to make a particular decision. Underlying this distinction is the democratic realist's belief that decision-making should be limited to the knowledgeable, and that those in authority are most likely to be authorities. We know that the two forms of authority are substantially independent. What people are searching for is the correct decision, and in their anxiety over making the decision they select persons in authority to do so.

The critics miss a crucial point. The practice of participatory democracy has an impact on the individual. Regardless of the outcome of a contested decision, participants are empowered, as well as educated, by the process.

What needs to be affirmed is that no decision-making process will guarantee the correct answer. However, giving a single person or set of persons the power to make decisions will guarantee the increasing likelihood of the wrong decision and lead to the alienation of those excluded from the process, right or wrong.

STEP ELEVEN

The path diverges. Either we choose the direction of institutional reform or we choose to work for radical change. In my view, all radicals are reformists but not all reformists are radicals. Most reformists are trapped in the ideological confines of the institution or society they seek to change. Their goal is to oust the incumbent regime, replacing it with themselves or their clones. Others work to replace the economic system while leaving the underlying social structures intact. Reformists are bound to the society in which they live. That is a major reason why the civil rights movement ground to a screeching halt. Radicals are antiauthoritarian, antibureaucratic, and antihierarchical, and are in but not of the society in which they live. However, distinguishing between reformism and radicalism is not always clear-cut.

Modern capitalist societies are extraordinarily flexible in co-opting or absorbing reforms so that they do not affect the prevailing distribution of power. Nevertheless, reformists are guided by two axioms. The first is the belief that reforms are cumulative: no matter how small, it all adds up. Second, these cumulative reforms take time: the byword is *gradualism*. These are expressions of a faith in the changeability of the system. I know of no empirical evidence to support these axioms.

STEP TWELVE

For All To Eat (FATE), a highly successful feeding program located in a poor city in a poor neighborhood almost equally populated by whites, blacks, and Latinos, fed an average of three hundred homeless or otherwise impoverished people every day. Although FATE's cadre were committed radicals, over a period of years they became concerned that their program, while a genuine social force in the community, was supporting a subculture of dependency. Despite their other work in the community, which included publishing a local newsletter and helping to maintain a laundromat, they observed a population that basically came to eat and run.

After much deliberation, the cadre decided that for people to eat at FATE, they would have to participate in some way in the food preparation and cleanup. What happened was unexpected. Ninety percent of those who came to eat dropped out. They were unable or refused to participate. The ten percent who remained became part of a new and expanded activist group.

In my perspective, the original FATE, as a soup kitchen, was barely something more than social welfare (nongovernmental organization). In its metamorphosis, it had begun a shift from passivity to reformism and perhaps to a radical stance.

STEP THIRTEEN

A less ambiguous case can be gleaned from following the issue of housing and segregation. Douglas Massey, a leading sociologist who has studied intensively the matter of housing segregation, put forward the following policy proposals. He called on the Department of Housing and Urban Development (HUD) to increase their assistance to local groups to deal with housing discrimination; to establish a more widespread and elaborate testing program; to scrutinize lending data and bank transactions; to increase enforcement of hate crimes, especially those related to housing; and to increase the funding and activities of HUD.

For those seriously committed to housing desegregation, it would be hard to reject these proposals, which are a genuine reformist platform and would likely make substantial changes in the ethnic composition of some neighborhoods, at least for a while. Let me counterpose some radical proposals. First we need to change the ownership and governance of communities by the use of land contracts and the development of community self-government. In doing so, we shift the power base away from HUD and the selling, lending, and insurance companies. We should encourage the design and construction of housing for the aged as well as housing for group and communal living. We should focus on the ecological balance of neighborhoods and fund the development of new technologies in housing construction and urban planning. Although I present both sets of proposals in outline, the differences in the reformist and radical agenda should be apparent. Central to the reformist proposal is the expansion of the responsibilities of the government and the planners, developers, and conventional real estate actors. Central to the radical proposals is the empowerment of residents; planning and development belongs to them.

STEP FOURTEEN

At various times throughout history, reformists and revolutionists have identified different locations as strategic to the establishment of a new political economy. Marx, for example, pointed to the working class while

Bakunin, his rival at the time, pointed to the unemployed and declassed. A century later, the New Left spoke of the new working class. Are some groups more likely than others to be in a vanguard for social change? I think not. Are there strategic sites, then, where one might do better at organizing people for change? Again, I think not. Rather, I think a radical intervention is more likely to succeed in certain times and places than others, but those opportunities are not immutable. At this moment in time, I look to three sites. Education is one. The issues of grade school and high school organization and teaching presently divide the political elites because their central intervention, "No Child Left Behind," and similar enrichment programs are failing. Further, the school systems most targeted in these programs are located in older central cities where the children are poor blacks and Latinos.

Some interventions that focus on self-help and mutual aid may work sometimes, such as the case of FATE (see the "Step 12" section) after it was refashioned. One unexplored and strategic group requiring assistance consists of people who have been victims of discrimination and ethnoviolence. I believe that at this time, self-help groups should be a major organizing tool for social change. It is an unmet need almost everywhere.

The third site in this trek is the news media. The mainstream press, as I have shown previously, is a major vehicle of stereotypes and perpetrator of discrimination. On that count alone, they are an important target. However, we need some way to tell our stories, and that is where the alternative press plays a critical role. Paper and electronic media are accessible at a level unprecedented in history. The Seattle-based Independent Media Center, for example, was started as a way to cover and broadcast the major demonstrations against the World Trade Organization in November 1999. Their organizing slogan was "Don't hate the media, be the media." Today there are over one hundred fifty IndyMedia centers across the world practicing a policy of open publishing on their news wire and participatory democracy in their organizational form.

STEP FIFTEEN

As agents of social change, we have a dual mission. To begin with, we need a sketch of the good society we are organizing towards. What kind of world do we envision? How do we structure equality in social institutions? Can we have nonhierarchical organizations? How do we structure a participatory economics? How is wealth distributed? How do we cope with crime? How do we educate our children in a nonauthoritarian fashion? Coming up with questions is easy, especially in this somewhat abstract manner. More difficult is our attempt at sketching answers. That's our first mission.

Our second, inextricably related mission is the way we live. It is not sufficient to dream our dreams. We need to try to live them. As a poet once wrote (I paraphrase), we must live as if we were in an experiment in the future.

NOTES

1. Francesca Polletta, *Freedom Is an Endless Meeting* (Chicago: University of Chicago Press, 2002), 233.

2. Robin Hahnel, *Economic Justice and Democracy* (New York: Routledge, 2005), 376.

INDEX